Foreword

My mother would often tell us stories of her life in a convent. As one who was brought up on the stories of Enid Blyton, it sounded to me like some sort of idyllic existence, akin to boarding school, where I imagined late night raids on the tuck shop, toasting bread by an open fire and lashings of ginger beer and cake.

As I grew older, it became obvious that this was not the case. As I listened to the underlying stories, it was apparent that life there was harsh. Conditions were poor and beatings were regular. In this modern age, the fact that some Catholic convents were places of physical and mental abuse is now well documented but in the 70s, when I started to become aware of the complex psyche of this former convent girl who was such an excellent parent, it was shocking and painful.

As I reflect upon the type of person my mother is, I'm acutely aware that she was deeply traumatised and affected by her past. She has spent a lifetime trying to be a 'good person' and yet, deep down, everything she does has to be seen to meet the approval of the nuns that raised her decades ago.

Many people have suggested that she document her time at Nazareth House and so she spent many years writing, by hand, her memories of life in Bexhill during the late 40s and through the 50s. Some of it is funny and some of it is tragic but I believe it has had a cathartic effect on her: she seems relieved to have finished it but I also think she's surprised to find out how many people are now waiting to read the final version.

If you ever get to read this book, I think you'll agree it's a childhood few of us would recognise. In this day and age we'd be talking of police action and social welfare but, back then, no one would have believed that nuns could be so cruel.

When you read of the torment the convent girls suffered, I think it's remarkable that any of them could have led normal lives and yet many of them married and had children. My mother was married to my father for over 50 years, something of which I am most definitely proud.

The convent is no longer there: it's now a common-or-garden housing estate - but the legacy of Nazareth House is far-reaching. There are many books available written by former convent girls and the stories of abuse at the hands of nuns is common, but it's important to note that not all nuns acted in a cruel or malignant way. Indeed, you will read that many of them were kind and nurturing and in fact my mother returned to the convent on many occasions after she had left to visit various people that had taught and raised her. I have happy memories of accompanying her on a few of those visits and she always seemed content upon leaving.

Let me close by simply saying: Mum. I'm so proud of you. When do you start the next book?

Mike Durham – August 2019

Chapter 1

"Phyllis?" I heard my aunt Floss calling me. "Can you go to the bottom of the garden and ask Uncle Bert to let you have two eggs? Bring them back here right away and don't you drop them."

I scurried to the end of the garden where Uncle Bert kept a few chickens. "Hello my dear," he said. "Have you come to see me?"

"Aunt Floss wants two eggs right away please," I said. "Oh right away is it," he said giving me a wink. "We'd better not keep her waiting then, had we? Here you are my dear and be careful not to break them."

I took the eggs, one in each hand, and walked very slowly and carefully back up the path. I had just about reached half way when the air-raid siren sounded. I jumped with fright and promptly dropped one of the precious eggs. Aunt Floss came running out of the back door. "Stupid child!" she yelled, flicking the wet tea towel across my bare legs as she retrieved the other egg from me. "Get into the shelter, quick."

I hurried into the Anderson shelter which had been constructed in the garden, and Uncle Bert joined us. "You broke one of the eggs then, my dear?" he said.

"Yes," I sobbed, as I rubbed my sore legs.

"Stupid child!" repeated aunt Floss. "I'll be glad when her sister gets back from school and takes her from under my feet."

"Don't be so hard on the child," said Uncle Bert. "After all, she's barely four years old."

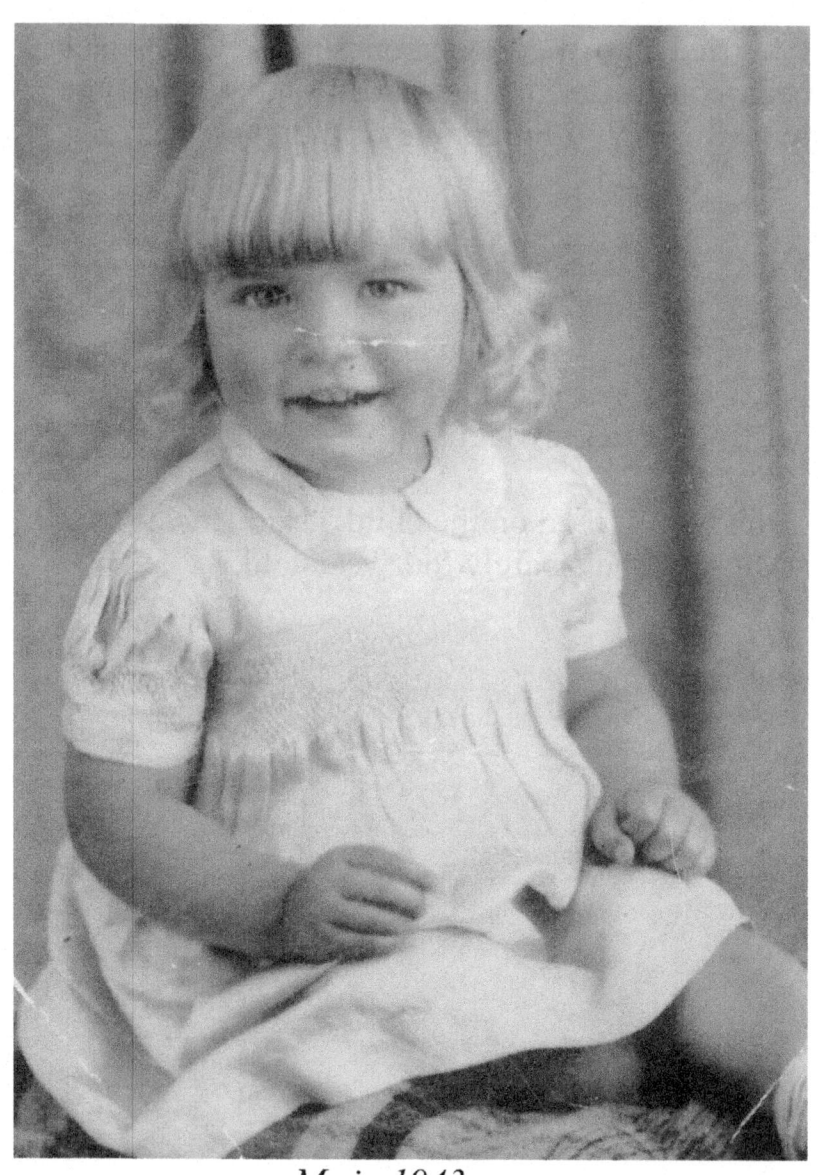
Me in 1943.

I could hear the noise of planes passing overhead. A huge bang sounded in the distance and the ground shook. "That was close," said Uncle Bert, puffing away on an empty pipe. Tobacco was scarce at the time but he still kept his pipe in his mouth as if it was full.

The "all clear" sounded and we left the shelter. Aunt Floss disappeared into the kitchen while Uncle Bert returned to his chickens. I stayed in the garden. It was a warm and sunny day and I lay on the grass picking daisies and waiting for my sister Lindy to get back from school. She would make the daisies into a pretty chain for me and put them around my neck and in my hair. I loved my sister so much and I hated it when she wasn't close by me.

I also had a brother whom I adored; his name was Alec and he was five years older than me. He was very clever and would point out the "dog-fights" going on in the sky and then do fantastic things with the bits of Perspex he would find after an air-raid: he would burn a hole in the Perspex with a hot poker and make rings and bracelets for me. Oh, he was so clever. No-one could climb a tree as fast as he could and he could catch the biggest frogs and newts and run the fastest. He was always out roaming and seldom stayed indoors so I didn't see him as much as I saw Lindy.

Alec, aged around 11.

We'd all three come to stay with Aunt Floss, Uncle Bert and their children in their house in

Cheam, Surrey. Our father was away fighting in the Second World War. He had left three weeks before I was born so I didn't know him. Aunt Floss said our mother was working away so she was looking after us for her. Aunt Floss was our mother's sister. We all used to live in Tooting, South London, but when war came we were on the move constantly.

I only had a very vague memory of my mother. I was outside in a play-pen watching my sister climbing a step ladder to pinch some apples from next door's tree. My mother was holding the step ladder while my sister did the stealing!

One night we were again out in the shelter during another raid. This time a bomb landed very close by and all the windows in the house were shattered. It was decided we would be evacuated. Uncle Bert stayed behind as he had a job to go to and he would need to look after the chickens: and so it was we found ourselves in South Molton in Devon.

Alec and Lindy were billeted with two separate families in town, while I was on a farm a couple of miles out of town with Aunt Floss and her children. I didn't see much of my beloved Lindy during that time; she had too much housework to do for the family she was staying with. Alec would come to see me though. He would chase the chickens on the farm into the pond to see if they could swim. We had great fun at harvest time watching the men cut the corn and put it into stooks; then a cart would come round to collect the stooks, pulled by two enormous Shire horses. Sometimes at the end of the day we'd be lucky enough to be given a ride on the backs of these gentle giants.

When the corn was being cut, rabbits would scurry here and there and one day my brother chased and caught one with his bare hands. It was killed and skinned for our dinner and Alec chased me all around the farm with the rabbit's innards.

If Alec wasn't around I would go into the little orchard and lay on the grass, watching the clouds scurrying about the sky. I was fascinated by clouds and could see pictures in them: a castle, a face, fairies. I spent many happy hours there.

Gradually, the days got shorter and the nights got longer and colder. I awoke one morning and was so surprised when I looked out of the window. Someone had got up into the sky and torn the clouds up! All the pieces were falling down and the ground was covered with them. I never realised that clouds were so cold.

When spring arrived the place was a sea of wild daffodils. Alec and I would pick armfuls and sell them in the town for 3d a bunch.

We were still in South Molton when the war ended. There was a big party in the street and Alec won a race on the scooter he'd built himself. My brother was so clever.

We eventually moved back again to Cheam. All the broken windows had been repaired but the chickens were nowhere to be seen. I asked Uncle Bert what had happened to them. "Well, my dear," he replied. "They all got fed up with the noise of airplanes and bombs, so they just flew away for a bit of peace and quiet!"

I was quite satisfied with this reply and skipped indoors for a nice chicken dinner. Later that evening, Aunt Floss sat and played the piano while Uncle Bert plucked away on his ukulele. I began to feel safer than I had for a long time, mainly because my Lindy was with me again.

Lindy always seemed to be beating mats or dusting or washing dishes. At these times I preferred to be in the garden helping Uncle Bert. When we heard the rag and bone man calling in the street, Uncle Bert would hand me the bucket and small shovel and send me onto the road to collect what the rag and bone man's horse had deposited. This was put onto the compost heap and I'm sure the horse knew that we collected it, because he always left a huge pile outside our house and no one else's.

Lindy's school wasn't too far away so I would often go down the road to meet her. One day she was walking along with a lady. When they saw me Lindy called out eagerly, "Phyllis, quick come and say hello!"

"Hello," I muttered shyly to the lady. "Don't you know who this is?" Lindy said. I shook my head as I looked at the lady. "This is Mummy and she's come to say goodbye."

"Goodbye," I said. As the lady kissed me on the cheek, I noticed she had a big tummy. She kissed Lindy then walked to the corner and disappeared around it without looking back.

"Mummy has to go away for a little while," said Lindy. She looked very sad so I put my hand in hers and told her Aunt Floss said she must be sure to do the washing up as soon as she got indoors.

One day as we were sitting on the front door step, Lindy was telling me what the sea-side was like. Alec was whittling away at a piece of wood with a pen knife he'd got by swapping cigarette cards. Suddenly, Lindy jumped up and yelled "Daddy, Daddy! Oh it's my Daddy". She flung herself into the arms of a very handsome soldier who came through the gate. "Phyllis, look, it's Daddy! He's come home at last!"

I went towards the man and was swept off my feet. I squealed and wriggled and I was thrown into the air and hugged and kissed. So this was my Daddy; Lindy had told me about him often. How he was a brave soldier who was fighting across the sea and how one day he would come home and we would all go back to our house in Tooting and be a proper family again.

"Look what I've got for you," said Daddy. He opened up his kit bag and handed me a lovely dolly. She was beautiful, with golden hair and a mauve dress.

"Where's yer manners? Say thank you!" I heard Aunt Floss say behind me. "Come through, Albert. I've got the kettle on." With that, my father walked on into the kitchen with Aunt Floss and the door closed.

I ran upstairs with my dolly. Lindy was trying on her new Swiss blouse. "And look at this Phyllis," she said excitedly. "It's a coral necklace. It's come from the bottom of the sea. Isn't it lovely to see Daddy again? What are you going to name your dolly?"

I'd learned a new word that very morning. I'd asked Lindy, "What's that?" as she put a spoonful of golden syrup on my Shredded Wheat at breakfast.

"Shhh," she said. "There's no sugar left so I'm putting a little bit of syrup on it to sweeten it."

I repeated the word. "Syrup! Syrup!" I liked the sound of it. "I'm going to call my dolly Syrup," I said, grandly.

"Syrup isn't a name!" said Alec, as he came into the room to show us the German helmet that Daddy had given him. (Thinking back - it could have been Dad's own helmet and not a German one.)

"I don't care!" I said. "I want to call her Syrup!"

"Well then: Syrup it is," said Alec as he sat my bottom into the helmet and spun me round and round. Lindy looked on, clapping her hands in delight. "We'll be going home soon," she laughed.

Daddy left, saying he would come and collect us in a couple of weeks and, sure enough, it seemed only a short time after that Aunt Floss called to us, "Come on children. Your father's here."

Lindy and Alec bounded down the stairs but I was frantically looking for Syrup. I looked everywhere: under the big bed we all three shared and inside the laundry basket in the bathroom. I went downstairs and looked under the cushions on the armchairs. "I can't find her!" I wailed.

"Never mind, dear" said Aunt Floss. "If I come across her, I'll send her on to you. Now off you go. Your Daddy's waiting."

On the way to the station Alec told me he'd seen Aunt Floss put Syrup into the dustbin. "But why?" I asked.

You'd left Syrup lying on the kitchen floor and Aunt Floss accidentally trod on her and broke her."

"The bitch!" I heard my Daddy say as he strode on towards the station. I had to run to keep up with them all.

"Are we going home?" I asked Daddy as we climbed aboard the big steam train.

"No. Your dear mother has sold everything and gone. Someone else lives there now."

"Where are we going then?" I looked at Lindy for reassurance.

"We're going to stay with Aunt Eva for a while," she said.

"Who is Aunt Eva?" I wanted to know.

Alec put his arm around me. "Aunt Eva is one of Daddy's sisters. You and Lindy are staying there while me and Daddy go into lodgings."

"Is lodgings close to Aunt Eva?"

I really didn't want to be separated from Alec.

"I won't be too far away," was his reply. I looked at Daddy but he was staring out of the window.

Lots of kids were out playing in the street as we walked up Honeybrook Road in Balham. Turning into number 20, alongside a neatly trimmed privet hedge, I was fascinated with the coloured tiles laid out in a lovely pattern on the path. In the middle was an iron cover where the coal would be delivered into the cellar below.

Aunt Eva greeted us all and we trooped inside where she handed round tomato sandwiches and cups of tea. She lived on the ground floor with

Uncle Des, her husband, and our cousins: Brian, Dennis and Patricia. Upstairs lived another of Daddy's sisters, Ann, and her husband, Len, along with daughter Julie.

Aunt Eva gave me a big hug and then spooned extra condensed milk into my tea. I liked her straight away. After we'd eaten, Alec, Brian and Dennis went off to explore the coal cellar. Lindy, Patricia and I went into the little back garden where they taught me how to skip using a piece of rope hacked off the end of Aunt Eva's washing line.

Daddy and Aunt Eva shut themselves in the sitting room for a talk. It must be ever so boring being a grown up, I thought. All they ever did was hide themselves away to talk.

We settled in quickly and I started school, although not the same one as Lindy. She wore a very smart navy-blue uniform with a badge showing the letters L.R. She explained that the letters stood for La Retreat, a school for Catholic girls. "I'm a Catholic and so are you," she informed me.

"So why can't I come to your school with you?" I wanted to know.

"You're not quite old enough yet," she replied. I couldn't wait to be the same age as my sister but, hard as I tried, I could never catch up.

She came home from school one day and announced she had made her first confession. This didn't mean a thing to my 5-year-old mind. She explained that she had to go into a Confessional Box and tell the priest all the naughty things she'd done. I was horrified. How could they both fit in the box? Did they put the lid down? Was it awfully dark in there? Besides, it was a terrible waste of time because Lindy never did anything naughty. She smiled and said I'd understand everything when I made my first confession. I dreaded the day.

I used to wonder why I and a few other pupils had to go out of the classroom when it was prayer time. "It's cos we're Caflicks," another girl told me. There was that word again. I began to feel important being a Catholic!

Alec would come over at the weekends and we'd go to the pictures on Saturday mornings, or get the underground train or bus to Clapham Common or Hyde Park. It was great fun in the parks where we would pick big fronds of ferns and tuck them in our belts to make grass skirts. Alec would sometimes bring a toy yacht and we'd spend hours sailing it from one side of the lake to the other. My brother was so clever at everything; he would get a stick and tie a string to it, then wrap the string around the stopper from a lemonade bottle. I would play 'whip the top' so contentedly.

He would make me lovely colourful kites with long tails and we'd fly them on the common. Once he got a 'y' shaped twig and lifted a complete spider's web from a hedge: it still had a spider in it! He showed me my first conker: I was fascinated with it and loved the dark shiny smoothness of it and I kept repeating the word 'conker' over and over again. I liked the sound of it.

In September 1945, I had my sixth birthday. Alec made me a tank out of a matchbox, cotton reels, candle and elastic bands. I was also given a brand new dolly. She was a beautiful dark brown and her face and head were so smooth and shiny I promptly named her... Conker.

Christmas came and, although things were still on ration, I remember a great Christmas party. Aunt Eva and Uncle Des must have scrimped and scraped to make it such a lovely time for us. We played games: someone blindfolded me and stuck my fingers in half an orange, then told me that I was feeling Lindy's brains where she'd fallen and cut her head open. I burst into floods of tears and Aunt Eva picked me up and cuddled me for a very long time. It was the first time I could ever remember being cuddled by a grown-up.

Dad would come over occasionally but he was always in a hurry and spent most of the time talking with Aunt Eva behind closed doors. He'd gone back to work in Hovis Flour Mills, the job he had before the war.

One day, Lindy and I were called into the sitting room with Aunt Eva. "I've something to tell you," she said. "You are both going to go and live by the sea."

I almost fell off the chair in my excitement. Lindy had told me all about the seaside and I'd seen pictures of it in my book. My sister put her arm around me. "Are we all going?" she asked.

"No," said Aunt Eva. "Just you and Phyllis."

"But what about Alec?" Lindy said.

"He'll be staying with your Dad for a while, just until we get something sorted out."

"Is it because we've been naughty, is that why we're being sent away?" Lindy's voice was trembling.

Aunt Eva put her arms around us both, "Oh, heavens, no!" she said. "I'd dearly love to keep you both here with us, but your Daddy wants you to be brought up in a Catholic home."

"Aren't you a Catholic then?" I asked my Aunt with pity.

"No, pet. Neither is your Daddy, that's the problem." She explained: "You see, when your Daddy married your Mummy, she was a Catholic and your Daddy had to make a promise that any children born would be raised as Catholics. So, being as your Mummy won't be back now, your Daddy has been to the Catholic Rescue Society to see if they could help. They say they have a place for you both down by the seaside."

"Why won't Mummy be coming back?" asked Lindy.

"Well, your Dad has decided to divorce her," answered Aunt Eva. "Listen, we won't say too much in front of Phyllis. We don't want to upset her, do we?"

"Can I take Conker with me?" I asked.

"Of course you can," was the answer. I hurried off to tell Conker all the news while Lindy stayed and talked some more with Aunt Eva.

About two weeks later we were ready to go. I don't remember saying goodbye to Alec or Daddy. It was Aunt Eva who had the job of taking us on the long journey to Bexhill on Sea in Sussex. The date was March 25th 1946.

Chapter 2

Nazareth House was a huge place set in its own grounds and consisted of three main buildings. The central building housed the community of about twenty nuns. Above that was the nursery, housing children from newly born babies to the age of five. Left of the central building was a department for ladies and, on the first floor, the chapel. A wing for men was situated to the rear of the central building.

Nazareth House, Bexhill-on-Sea.

To the right was the children's wing and this was to be my home until my school days were over. The sheer size of the place was daunting and I held very tightly to Lindy with one hand and onto Conker with the other. We walked up to the front door and were greeted by a lady who ushered us into a parlour where we waited for a nun. I had never seen a nun before and when one arrived, dressed from head to toe in black, I was a bit frightened. The only other people I knew who dressed all in black were witches. I know, 'cos I saw them in my picture book.

Nuns or witches? These are the habits they would wear.

There was a knock on the door and a lady entered with a large tray of tea and sandwiches. We sat and ate as the nun asked Aunt Eva lots of questions and wrote everything down in a book.

Aunt Eva had tears in her eyes as she left. We were then taken to the children's wing where Lindy had to join the senior girls and I was taken into the juniors' classroom. Sister Ann Mary came towards me and held my hand. "I'm Catholic and I've come to live by the seaside and Conker has come with me," I gabbled on as I looked around the room. Thirty pairs of eyes looked at me, all girls of about the same age.

"That's nice dear," said Sister Ann Mary. "Let me have your doll; she will have to stay in this cupboard with all the rest of the dolls until it's play time. Hang your coat on that peg and remember your number is 54." She had a very soft voice with an Irish accent. She handed me a slate with some chalk, gave me a smile and said, "Draw me a nice picture."

I settled down to do some drawing, desperately wishing Lindy was near me. A bell rang shortly after. "Collation time," Sister said. We were filed out along a passage with red quarry tiles and into the refectory for our tea. I spotted Lindy as she came in with the senior girls. We stood together as everyone else went to their allotted tables.

"I've been drawing and Conker's in a cupboard," I told her.

Who's talking?" asked a nun who had followed us into the refectory.

"The new girls," someone said and we were pointed out. The nun turned and looked at us. There was something about those cold piercing eyes that frightened me. This was Sister Columba and she was in charge of the seniors.

She pointed to a table with two spaces. "You two sit there," she said, "and know that talking is not allowed in the refectory unless I give you permission." I went to sit down but was grabbed by Sister Columba. "You haven't said your 'Grace' yet, young lady," she said, sternly.

I stood again and faced towards the big crucifix on the wall, like everyone else was doing. We asked God to bless the meal we were about to receive and to bless our benefactors. (I remembered thinking that I must ask Lindy who Benny Factors was.)

We sat in silence and ate the slice of stale bread that had been scraped with the most appalling spread I'd ever tasted. I drank the cup of milk then stood again to thank God for what we'd eaten.

And so I settled into the routine of life in the convent. I would only see Lindy at meal or play times but she would always find a way of hurriedly and covertly coming into the junior dormitory to tuck me in and kiss me goodnight.

There were between eighty and a hundred girls in the convent, whose ages ranged from five to fourteen years. When you reached fourteen, if you didn't have a home or job to go to, you joined the group of girls known as the 'exes'. They would work in the convent in various departments such as the laundry, kitchen, nursery, linen room or in the old peoples' departments. There were about a dozen or so exes at any one time; some were orphans and, if they could not get a job on the outside, they just stayed in the convent right into old age. Most of them did find outside work though, with the nuns' help, and left to make their own way in life.

A lot of the children were orphaned because of the war - a few were just abandoned in the convent - but the majority at least had someone to call their own.

The routine was harsh compared to today's standards of living. A typical day would start at 6.15 am when one of the nuns would wake us by clapping her hands together or ringing a bell. You would have to jump out of bed and get straight onto your knees to offer your day to God. Then you stood at the end of your bed and stripped off all the bedclothes, which you folded neatly and put on the chair beside your bed. You then all filed into the washrooms, still keeping the silence, while one of the exes went round to examine the beds to make sure no one had wet theirs. After dressing and more morning prayers you would make your way through the central building for morning Mass.

After Mass, it was back to the children's wing for breakfast which was either a bowl of porridge or a sausage in a plateful of grease. I looked in astonishment during my first breakfast as two girls stood eating their meals with sheets over their heads. This was the fate that befell you if you dared to wet your bed. When breakfast was over and 'Grace' had been said, you were allowed to speak.

Everyone in the seniors had an allotted task to do, e.g. washing up; sweeping and polishing the refectory, the three classrooms, the passages and dormitories; making sure all the castors on the beds were facing the same way; etc. Baths, washbasins and lavatories had to be cleaned out daily. Six girls would go to clean the chapel - sweeping, dusting, waxing and polishing benches, pews and floors on hands and knees.

The juniors would be out playing while the seniors were working. Most playtimes were organised for juniors; if it was a fine day, we would form a ring in the big playground and sing songs or play ring games. We were not allowed to sit and watch because, "The Devil finds work for idle hands to do."

At 8.55 am a bell would summon every girl to her classroom where school started with the rosary and a hymn, followed by half an hour of religious education. At 10.30 there would be a milk break and then it was back to lessons until it was time for dinner.

When the washing up was done after dinner and the refectory swept and tables laid for the next meal, we'd go out for a walk in a 'crocodile line' if it was fine: then back for afternoon lessons. After collation, there was benediction in the Chapel and then play until supper.

Straight after supper, we juniors would go for a strip wash or bath, brush teeth, brush hair (one hundred strokes!), kneel down for night prayers then hop into bed, arms crossed over the chest. I was told this was in case you died in your sleep, in which case you'd already be 'laid out'.

The first time I had a bath I found myself in the water with what appeared to be half a sheet. I sat there and waited for an ex-girl to come in and bath me. When she came in she gasped and said, "Put that bath gown on at once". With that she picked up the sheet, which was a square with two slits for your arms to go through; this covered your front so that you nor anyone else would be able to see your naked body. I was duly bathed then wrapped in a bath sheet and carried out and placed on a huge bath mat with five other newly-bathed girls. We would dry ourselves while those waiting to be bathed sat on benches, folding their flannels into doll shapes and then wrapping them up in bath towels. This was how we amused ourselves while Sister sat in the corner cutting the finger or toenails of those who needed it.

One day, Lindy told me that Daddy had written and told her that Alec was now in a convent for boys in Gravesend, Kent. This upset me a lot as he would be there without knowing anyone. At least I had Lindy to comfort me when I needed it but who would Alec have?

My last thoughts before I went to sleep that night were of Alec and I asked Jesus to please look after him. I awoke when it was very dark and I froze in terror: my bed was saturated. What could I do? I'd have to wear the sheet on my head at breakfast and be called a "dirty piss-pot" by the other girls. I decided I must go to Lindy and ask her to help me. I crept into the senior dormitory and tiptoed past rows of sleeping girls. I wasn't even sure if I could remember where Lindy's bed was. I did eventually find it (under a big picture of Saint Don Bosco) and I shook her awake. She was out of bed like a shot and, before I knew it, the offending sheet was off my bed and put on one of the radiators to dry. She re-made my bed and tucked me in and promised she'd be up before anyone to retrieve my sheet and no one would be any the wiser. True to her word, the sheet was back in the morning but, when my bed was inspected, a huge stain was spotted and I was found out.

Oh, the humiliation of that breakfast. Poor Lindy tried so hard to console me but nothing helped. I was now labelled a 'bed-wetter' and would have to endure a huge brown rubber sheet over my mattress complete with my number 54 written on it in indelible ink. Also, my night time drink of cocoa would be halved - I would join the rank of girls known as 'the wet beds' who were not allowed a full one. From then on I was scared to go to sleep in case it happened again, which sometimes it did.

Christmas came and what an exciting time that was. All the decorations in the playroom and refectory were made by the seniors. Our junior classroom had paper chains that had been made by us and on the walls were pictures that we had coloured. For weeks we had been learning the words and tunes to various carols: we were so excited.

We got up for Midnight Mass, which was sung in Latin by the school choir. The chapel was crowded and there was a life size crib. The smell of the candles and incense along with the beautiful singing almost moved me to tears. I just wished Alec was with us and then I would have been perfectly happy. I thought of him as I got back into bed after Mass, but was terrified to sleep in case I wet the bed again.

I kept hoping that Father Christmas wouldn't forget to visit Alec. Did Father Christmas know where Gravesend was? I didn't even know where Gravesend was! "Please Jesus, show Father Christmas the way to Gravesend and let Alec know how much I miss him."

I eventually drifted off into a fitful sleep. When I woke, I found that we juniors each had a new pair of knee length socks to put on. Our old ones had been stitched together at the open end and hung over a rope that had been stretched across the playroom. We hurriedly prayed, washed and dressed and ran down to the playroom to find that Father Christmas had been and filled our stockings with goodies. There was an apple in the toe of one sock and an orange in the other. Then there were nuts, a colouring book, crayons and a skipping rope. Oh! I was so happy.

We went up to the refectory for a feast of a breakfast; bacon and eggs and fried bread, made all the better because we were allowed to speak during the meal.

When the washing up was done and the beds were made, the seniors joined us in the playroom. Father Christmas arrived and handed everyone their parcels (which had been kept safely over the past few weeks). Those who had no one to send them gifts had parcels made up for them by the nuns... no one was left out. Lindy and I shared a parcel from Daddy. It contained some comics and sweets and in an envelope was a 5/- postal order. We were rich! But not for long. Someone came around and collected all the money that was received to pay for the new socks we were wearing!

I wanted to go and ask father Christmas if he'd been to see Alec yet, but Lindy said not to: he'd have to rush off to Africa soon because it was still night there.

Time passed by and Sister Ann Mary was replaced by Sister Magdalen. She would sometimes read us stories when we were tucked up in bed: a real treat. She was also a very good teacher and made most of the lessons enjoyable. Sister Columba still had charge of the seniors and she was very strict: everyone seemed to fear her and she was very quick to use the cane if you stepped out of line. One breakfast time a girl dropped her plate of porridge and Sister Columba made her pick the bits of china out and then eat the porridge. "Waste not, want not."

When everyone was in the playground, the juniors no longer had to be in a ring, so I could talk and play with whoever I liked. I had a good circle of friends my own age and we would often talk together. One day, a group of us were playing five-stones with our favourite pebbles when my friend Cindy asked me, "Have you got any people?"

"I've got a Dad," I said.

"Where's your Mum?" she wanted to know.

"She had to go away."

"Where to?" asked Clare, another friend "I don't know, but I'll ask my sister". With that I skipped over to Lindy "Where did Mum go to?" I asked.

She stopped playing hopscotch with the girls she was with, gave them a wink and said, "Mum was stolen by gypsies and they ate her."

I dashed back to my friends and told them. "Ugh, that's disgusting!" said Ann. "I knew they ate hedgehogs, but I didn't know they ate people."

"Someone said that there were gypsies camped in that field over there" said Yvonne, pointing to the field that backed onto our playing area.

"We'd better all keep together then!" Teresa said, as we joined Bridget, who was picking and eating 'bread and cheese' from the hawthorn hedge. This hedge, along with a row of tall poplar trees, separated our playground from a huge meadow in which we played when the summer came. There were two swings and a see-saw and we'd have a lovely time picking buttercups, making daisy chains and eating sorrel and vetch. When the grass grew really high, we'd tie clumps of grass together and would roll about with laughter when someone got their foot caught in it and fell over. In a part of this meadow, out of bounds to us, there was a huge old oak tree with a wooden hut close by. The babies and toddlers from the nursery would play under the tree and have a nap in the hut, watched over by a nun and a couple of exes.

Lindy called me one day and said, very excitedly, "Daddy's coming to visit us this Sunday."

I could hardly wait although I couldn't remember what he looked like. I told everyone, "I've got my people coming on Sunday."

"Lucky thing!" said Bridget "Don't forget, if you get any sweets, I'm your best friend."

"Don't your people come to see you then?" I asked her.

"I haven't got any people" she said.

"Where are they then?"

"Don't know."

"I've got a Mum," said Cindy, "but I don't know about my Dad."

"Same as me," said Clare. "My Mum's in Brighton but I haven't got a Dad"

"I've got a Dad and I think I've got a Mum, but I think they've lost me." Valerie, wearing glasses, looked at me out of her one good eye, her other covered by a plaster. She'd just lost a tooth as well and she looked so peculiar.

"I expect the police will tell them you're here," said Teresa, kindly.

"I hope so," replied Valerie. "I'm fed up with wearing these button-up knickers. I want proper knickers with elastic in them. The buttons keep coming off mine and I can't find a safety pin." With that she ran off to skip, with her knickers falling around her ankles.

"Poor creature," Yvonne said. "I don't think she's got any people."

My Dad arrived about 2 o'clock that Sunday afternoon, after we'd been waiting impatiently for what seemed like hours. He arrived in his army uniform and looked a very handsome figure. Unfortunately, it was raining and we couldn't go out so we sat in the visitors' parlour and talked. He said he would tell us a secret but we were not to tell the nuns. "I've married Aunt Margaret," he said very quietly.

I looked at Lindy: she was clapping her hands. "Oh good!" she said. "So when can we come home?"

"Hang on," he said. "You won't be able to. For a start Aunt Margaret, your step-mother, has a very responsible job that she can't give up and we only rent a very small one-bedroomed flat - and besides, the landlord says we are not permitted to have children living there."

"Oh." I could hear the disappointment in Lindy's voice. "I'm due to leave school soon and I was hoping to get a job."

"Do you know what you want to do?" asked Dad.

"I'd rather like to work with children," Lindy replied.

"I'll have a word with the nuns," he said. "Now, what are your favourite sweets? They're still on ration but I'm sure we can send you some."

We talked some more then Dad said he'd have to leave or he would miss the London train. He kissed us and gave us 6d each and then left, promising that next time he came he'd bring our new mother.

I just could not work this out. I joined my friends. "What is an Aunt?" I asked Ann.

"It's either your Mum or your Dad's sister," she replied.

That's just what I thought. Now, I knew my Mum had a sister called Floss, but she didn't have one called Margaret. A dreadful thought came to me. "Oh my gosh. My Dad must have married one of his sisters. It's no wonder he wanted us to keep it a secret from the nuns."

"Oh, that's a sin," Cindy looked at me gravely.

"Yes, it's a mortal sin," said Yvonne. "If he dies, he'll go to hell straight away."

I ran to Lindy, sobbing my heart out. "Dad will go to hell 'cos he's married one of his sisters."

"Aunt Margaret is not one of Dad's sisters," she explained. "She's just someone we call 'aunt'. Don't you remember her?"

"No," I answered with great relief.

"Anyway, why are you telling people about this? Dad said it was a secret."

"He only said we weren't to tell the nuns," I said defensively.

Chapter 3

It was 1947. Spring came and we'd go out for a walk 'crocodile' fashion each afternoon. To get to the road we'd have to pass by a small green hut erected under two horse chestnut trees by the main gate. S sat in this hut would invariably be Mr. Houlihan, smoking his pipe and accompanied by his two dogs, Bonzo, a black Spaniel, and Spider, a Jack Russell Terrier. The dogs would like to come over and sniff at us as we went by but a few of the children were afraid of dogs and this often led to almost panic amongst them.

One day, I chummed with Valerie as my walking partner; she was clutching at her waist. "What's wrong?" I asked her.

"Nothing, it's just that my button has come off my knickers again," she explained.

As we neared the green hut, Bonzo came over to sniff at Valerie, who happened to be one of those who was terrified of dogs. She tried to hide behind me but Bonzo must have thought she wanted to play, because he kept coming. With that, Valerie turned to run and, with a high-pitched shriek, she let go of her waist: her knickers promptly fell around her ankles. She took a step forward and went sprawling down on the grass, her glasses flying off in the process. Bonzo, thinking this must be a great game, grabbed hold of the knickers and pulled with all his might. Children scattered left and right, some in fits of laughter. Valerie kicked off her knickers and Bonzo ran into the hut with them, shaking his head from side to side and growling playfully.

The two nuns who were accompanying us on the walk restored some sort of order. They had a word with Mr. Houlihan, who retrieved Valerie's knickers. She was sent back to the sewing room to have another button sewn on while we continued with our afternoon walk. We walked down to the beach at Glyne Gap, up over the cliffs and then back home again. I loved the seaside and couldn't wait for the warmer weather to come so we could go down and bathe.

When we got back to the main gate, all the children who were afraid of dogs were made to go and stroke Bonzo and Spider. Most of them found, to their delight, just how friendly they were. Ann however just could not bring herself to touch them. She shook with fear and refused to go anywhere near them. Later that evening, she was told to wait in the classroom. She was wondering what she had done wrong when the door opened quietly. Bonzo was pushed in and the door was closed behind him. Ann told us afterwards how she had immediately screamed and jumped on top of a desk. She continued screaming in terror for a good minute or so while Bonzo just looked at her then lay down quietly. When Ann found that she was not going to be eaten, she slowly got down from the desk and went inch by inch towards the now sleeping Spaniel and when Sister Columba went in there after ten minutes, Ann was discovered sitting on the floor beside Bonzo and stroking his head.

"We're going on a trip," someone shouted "We'll be going in a charabanc."

"What's a charabanc?" I asked Lindy.

"They are not called charabancs any more. They are coaches, like big buses but used for day-trips and lots of people can get on them."

"Where are we going?"

"We're going to Eastbourne for the day."

We didn't know where or how far Eastbourne was but it sounded like we were going to have a great time. The days leading up to "The Trip" were filled with threats: if we misbehaved, we would not be going. Everyone was on their best behaviour.

On the morning of the big day, Valerie was looking very down in the mouth. "What's wrong?" I asked.

"The button's come off my knickers again and I can't find it," she wailed. "I won't be able to go."

"Where did you lose it?"

"Don't know. It just came off."

A brilliant idea came to me. Where the button had come off, there was a hole. I had a length of wool that I was saving to play cat's cradle with so I threaded one end of the wool through the hole and the other end through the corresponding button hole. I tied a knot and a bow and - hey presto - the knickers stayed up.

"Thank you!" she said, with a huge sigh of relief.

Not one but two coaches arrived and each one was filled with equal numbers of seniors and juniors. Unfortunately it was Sister Columba who got on my coach but I wasn't going to let that spoil my day. Lindy couldn't go as she had been asked to help out in the nursery so I sat next to Margaret, a junior who was the same age as me. She looked very pale.

"Are you alright?" I asked. "I don't feel very well; I've got a tummy ache."

"Shall I tell Sister?"

"No, she might send me back and I'll miss the trip."

The coaches started up and we were off. "Can we sing?" someone asked.

"Please do," answered the driver. We sang all the songs that we had been practicing for a forthcoming concert. The driver was highly delighted and told Sister that he had never heard such young children sing so well. Sister was very pleased.

I looked at Margaret and said, "Pooh! What's that awful smell?"

"I think I've messed myself," she said, bursting into tears.

We were just pulling up at the seafront in Eastbourne. Someone had relayed the news back to Sister Columba. She came up to Margaret and pulled her roughly out of the seat. "You disgusting little trollop!" she said. "Get down into that sea and wash yourself off!"

Margaret got into the water, which was quite rough. She removed her knickers and rinsed them out in the sea.

"Kneel down and clean yourself!" shouted Sister.

The poor girl knelt in the water with her dress around her waist; she was sobbing and turning blue with cold. One of the seniors was sent to help her clean herself.

"You dirty slut!" said the senior. "Why didn't you go to the lavatory before you came out? Now I'll be going around smelling as bad as you!"

A public convenience was found and everyone was made to go. Then we walked up and down the sea front and listened to a brass band playing. After that, we all sat on the beach while sandwiches were passed around. We had brought an old pram along with us which held a churn of milk and plastic cups. A wooden box held the sandwiches, although "sandwiches" was too good a word to describe what we were given. It was two pieces of stale bread stuck together with the foul tasting margarine and with a scrape of greengage jam. A cup of milk completed our picnic.

The two nuns disappeared to eat their food: they never ate in front of us. Those children that were brave enough were allowed to go in for a paddle. All dresses had to be tucked inside knickers. Of course, Valerie had to be one of the ones who wanted a paddle. No sooner was her dress tucked into her knickers when the wool holding her together gave way: there was no such thing as nylon wool in those days. She was half way down the shingle when her drawers dropped around her ankles and she went sprawling head first, just as a big wave broke on the shore. Her hair was saturated but she managed to save her glasses being swept away and so, with her glasses in one hand and her knickers in the other, she ran back up to where we were all having hysterics at her expense. A senior told us not to be so unkind and then someone broke their shoelace in two and gave her half to 'mend' her knickers again.

Then it was back to the coaches and home again - singing all the way. We all agreed it was a lovely trip and one senior girl was picked to go and say "Thank you" to the nuns for such a lovely day.

That November, Princess Elizabeth married Prince Philip. Newspaper cuttings were posted onto the walls and we marvelled at the length of the bride's train. She looked so radiant and happy. I scanned the pictures of soldiers who were on parade, just in case my Daddy was there.

"It must be wonderful to be a princess and to marry a handsome prince," said Mavis.

June said, "There's a prince who lives in my house!"

"Dirty liar! There never is!" Mavis said.

"It's true. My dog is called Prince," laughed June.

"Oh you big dope!" said Mavis, and they both chortled at the joke.

Christmas came around again and once more we gave a concert. I had a small part in the nativity play. I was chosen to play a shepherd boy who worshipped at the crib. I carried a lit candle inside a glass container hanging on a shepherd's crook. When the play was over I went to lift up the lid to blow out the candle and yelled with pain at the heat of it. A big blister appeared on my finger and I went crying to Sister Magdalen.

"My finger's burned," I wailed.

"Oh don't be such a baby. Offer your suffering up to God because he suffered more pain than that for you," was the reply.

It's alright for God, I thought. He could magic his pains away if he wanted to, but I was hurting. Lindy came to kiss me goodnight and she looked at my blister. She tried to rub some soap on it but it still hurt like mad and I cried myself to sleep.

Our food didn't improve much. Dinner would consist of a lump of fatty meat, potatoes boiled in their skins and soggy cabbage complete with boiled caterpillars, slugs and earwigs. Puddings were usually semolina, tapioca or sago all made with water, not milk. Collation was the obligatory bread and scrape with a cup of milk and supper was usually crackly and crunchy bits of a pig's anatomy complete with jaw bones and teeth. We got quite a liking for this and accepted it as there was nothing else. One has to remember, of course, that this was just after the Second World War and food was still on ration.

Now and again we might have a boiled egg for supper, but that was very rare. Pigs and chickens and a few geese were kept at the convent and we'd often try to sneak up to the chicken run or the pig sty, just to see them. Sometimes when we were in church we could hear the pigs squealing as they were sent to be slaughtered. It was a good sound to hear, because we knew we might be getting home made sausages - but it was usually black pudding with great lumps of fat in it.

I think the whole convent was run on charity. There used to be two nuns whose job was to go around begging for money, clothes or food for the "poor little orphans". Sometimes stale cakes would appear, probably from a baker. They were usually buns, coconut slices or custard tarts and sometimes we'd find squashed cigarettes in the cakes but we would just pick out the pieces and eat the cakes quite happily.

In summer, our bread room was often infested with ants. We'd bang the bread on the table (which would sometimes shatter the bread into pieces) to dislodge the ants (which we'd squash into the table cloth) then scrape on the dreaded marge and tuck in. The margarine tasted so bad that I would put salt on my bread to blot out the taste and I have enjoyed an unhealthy lifetime of loving salt sandwiches since then.

"Special" margarine.

One dinner time, we had a change from cabbage: on our plates were butterbeans. I'd never had them before and I can't say I was overjoyed at the taste. They were very gritty and I pushed them to the side of my plate.

"Eat those beans up," Sister Columba said as she passed by me.

"I can't Sister. They taste all dirty and gritty."

She stopped and came back towards me. "You will eat them," she said very quietly, "or there will be no pudding for you."

This didn't bother me too much as I wasn't all that keen on 'frogs spawn'.

Everyone had finished eating and we all stood to give thanks to God for our food. As we were filing out I was grabbed by my hair and pulled back into the refectory.

"Don't think you are going anywhere until you've finished your meal," said Sister Columba.

"I can't!" I started to cry. "They make me sick".

"Is that so?" she said, beckoning three girls to come over. Two took hold of my arms while the third held my head from behind. Sister began spooning the beans into my mouth. I gagged and vomited into the plate but she just kept on piling the beans and vomit into my mouth until I kept it all down.

"There are plenty of starving people in the world who would gladly eat the good food that you get!"

I rejoined the juniors, crying my eyes out. Lindy came to me and put her arms around me. "She's a big bully!" I cried to my sister.

"Hush, dear," she said. "Try to be a good girl or you might be given the cane."

Lindy had already had a taste of the cane from Sister Columba for some now forgotten misdemeanour. She had brought the cane down so hard on Lindy's hand that she wasn't able to move her thumb properly from that day on.

I cried at the injustice of it all. Was this what Jesus meant when he said, "Suffer little children to come unto me."? If so, it was right - I was suffering.

Chapter 4

Six of us girls were receiving instructions for our first confession and Holy Communion. We'd been shown the confession box which was nothing like I'd imagined when Lindy told me of her first confession. We were walking back to the children's wing and reached the red tiled passage where two seniors were scrubbing it on their knees.

"You can't walk on this until it's dry," one of them said. The other girl went into the changing room and collected two towels. She threw them at us and said, "Dry the floor while you're waiting."

Not knowing what to do, I got on the floor and started rubbing it with one of the towels. "Not like that you big dope! Do the same as her."

I looked at Bridget who was making a draught by twirling the towel round and round like a windmill. The floor was drying as we watched it and, when it was dry enough, we were allowed to walk over it on tip-toe. The towels were returned and we were told to re-join the juniors.

"I must see my Aunt first," I said.

"Yes, I'm dying to go too," said Helen, and we headed towards the six lavatories. They were through a door leading off of the red passage. This door was never allowed to be shut. I went into the farthest lavatory as Helen disappeared into the first. Whilst in the lavatory the big door slammed shut and we didn't think anything of it but on leaving we walked straight into Sister Columba.

"Why was this door shut?" she asked, her eyes narrowing.

"Don't know, Sister," said Helen.

"It just slammed shut," I said.

Her hand went into her large right hand pocket and I knew we were in for it, but I didn't know what for.

"You two were up to low tricks, weren't you?" she said, a stick now in her hand.

I looked at Helen and she looked at me. We hadn't a clue as to what she was talking about.

"Come on, own up," she shouted. "You were doing low tricks, weren't you?"

"No, Sister. We only went to the toilet."

"So you're not only the lowest of the low, but liars too," she yelled as she brought the stick down onto each of us in turn. She didn't stop hitting us until we were both crying. "Get with the rest of the juniors."

She followed us as we went into the playroom. Suddenly it went very quiet as everyone saw us crying. "These two," she shouted for all to hear, "were caught doing low tricks in the six lavatories and they have been caned for doing so. We do not tolerate those sorts of actions. Now get on with your recreation."

She pushed us towards the rest of the juniors and play went on as she went to talk to the ex-girl who was looking after the kids.

"What were you doing?" asked one girl.

"We weren't doing anything," we said, still sobbing. "We were just coming out of the lavatories and bumped into her."

"Yes you were! You're dirty low creatures!" said another girl.

When the day came for our first confession I was reminded to confess my sin. I entered the confessional and made the sign of the cross. It was a bit spooky as I knelt and spoke into a small mesh window where I could just see the faint outline of a priest sitting sideways on to me.

"Bless me father for I have sinned. This is my first confession," I said, hoping I was saying everything right as I'd been taught. "I accuse myself of telling lies, having bad thoughts, being jealous of another girl, not paying proper attention at mass and (gulp) I was doing low tricks."

"Doing what?" said the priest.

"Low tricks, father."

"What are low tricks? Explain."

"I don't know father, but me and another girl got the cane for it."

"You must know what you were doing. You don't get caned for nothing. If you don't tell me, I can't absolve you of your sins." It went quiet - I didn't know what to say. "Now, where were you when you were caught doing these low tricks?"

"We were coming out of the lavatories."

"Ah. Did you lift her skirt up, or perhaps pull her knickers down?" he suggested.

"No father!" I said, quite indignantly.

"My child, you must have done something on those lines or you would not have got the cane."

"Yes, father," I said, thinking to myself, "I'd better go along with this. He's a priest and I'm only eight."

"So which was it?" he asked.

"I lifted her skirt," I lied. I just wanted to get out of that dark place.

"Very well child. Remember; never be afraid of telling a priest your sins. Now say the act of contrition."

"Oh my God, because you are so good I am very sorry for having sinned against you, and with the help of Your grace, I will try not to sin again," I intoned, my cheeks flaming.

"I absolve you - in nomine Patri et Filio et Spiritui Sancto," said the priest "Now say two 'Our Fathers' and two 'Hail Marys' for your penance."

I left the confessional and knelt in the chapel to say my penance. I really spoke to God and asked him to make me a better person. Now I felt all nice and clean inside. No sins on my soul. I must be sure to keep my soul clean because we six were making our First Communion in the morning during Sunday Mass.

It was great to be a First Communicant: you were allowed to wear your white dress, shoes and socks all day long. You could go anywhere in the convent that you wanted to, barring the nuns' quarters, of course. There was a special table laid up for you with goodies and a big fuss was made of you all.

Going to sleep that night, I examined my conscience to make sure I hadn't committed any more sins, but I asked God to forgive me again, just in case I'd missed anything out. Lindy came to kiss me goodnight and gave me a Holy Picture of Our Lady. I put it in my prayer book then went to sleep. I still have that picture.

The Holy Picture given to me by Lindy.

We dressed in our white dresses the next morning and Sister put on our veils. She reminded us of the do's and don't's and then we were in church, kneeling in the very front pew for all to see. A lot of outside people would come in for Sunday Mass and we were delighted that so many people were there to see us six take our First Communion.

The time came and we filed up to the altar rails and knelt in a row. The priest handed the communion plate to the first girl who put it under her chin with both hands. She put out her tongue while the priest gently laid the Sacred Host onto her tongue saying (in Latin), "Receive the Body of Christ". The plate was then passed onto the next girl and so on until all six of us had received God into our hearts and souls. We then stood and turned with both hands joined in prayer and walked slowly back to the front pew.

We were supposed to keep our eyes downcast but I wanted to see if my sister was watching, and I searched for her. I looked straight into the angry eyes of Sister Columba and quickly lowered my gaze again.

I knelt and thanked Jesus for coming into my heart while everyone else filed up for their communion. I can remember feeling disappointed because nothing happened inside me. I was expecting a warm, holy glow or something - but I just felt the same as before. I could hardly wait for Mass to finish then so that we could get down to our "Communion Breakfast".

Just as we were finishing out breakfasts, Reverend Mother Superior came into the refectory. Everyone stood up and said, "Good Morning Reverend Mother."

"Good morning, girls" she said. I'd never seen her before because she rarely came into our wing. She walked towards our table and said, "How are our First Communicants then?" She smiled and handed each of us a small medal on a blue ribbon which we put around our necks. "This is a very special day for each of you girls, so try to remember and enjoy every minute of it."

"Oh, thank you, Reverend Mother," said Sister Columba in a voice we'd seldom heard her use before. "The girls have just finished breakfast. Would you do us the honour of saying grace?"

We all stood and faced the crucifix and said our thanks to God. We six were told we could go anywhere but to keep together and not to do anything to disgrace ourselves.

Our first port of call was to go past the laundry and drying grounds and around the corner to where the chickens were kept in a big run. There was a nun in there feeding them. She saw us and smiled.

"Hello, girls. Do you want to come inside and help me feed them?"

We scampered inside and Sister let us each throw a handful of food to the chickens milling around us. Yvonne opened the wire gate into the next run to throw her handful of feed in there.

"Watch out for the cockerel," Sister started but it was too late! This enormous cockerel threw himself at Yvonne who beat a hasty retreat back with us. Sister laughed, and so did we. It was so nice to be with a friendly nun.

"Can we go and see the pigs, please Sister?"

"Yes of course, I've already fed them so I won't come with you."

Away we went, chatting excitedly. It was great to be a First Communicant.

"Pooh, don't they smell?" said Pat.

"Yes, but aren't they nice?" I answered. The smell reminded me of being with Aunt Floss when we were evacuated to the farm in Devon.

"I dare you to go in there," said Julie.

"They won't hurt you," I replied.

"Prove it then, go in there!"

"Alright!"

I slid back the bolt and I was about to pick my way in when I was pushed from behind. My white plimsoll went straight into a great dollop of pig shit. The other five ran off shrieking with laughter. I got outside the pen and re-bolted it. I shook and shook my foot but, oh, what a mess. I limped back to the children's wing to find my sister. "Look what they did to me," I sobbed to her.

"Never mind, sweetheart. Don't cry on your First Communion day. It's unlucky." She washed off the offending muck then blancoed my plimsoll. All was well again and I went off to find the other five. I found them in Timber Passage, frightened to go past a big statue of the Virgin Mary.

"Mickey's hiding behind there and he jumps out every time we try to go past," said Bridget, pointing to a tiny black and white kitten waiting to pounce. Now was my chance for revenge. I got behind Yvonne and gave her a shove forward. Mickey jumped out, his little legs pointing north, south, east and west. Yvonne shrieked while the rest of us ran past, followed quickly by Yvonne. Mickey took up his place behind the statue again, waiting for the next unsuspecting person.

"We're going to the nursery to see the babies," said Helen. I was delighted to hear this as Lindy would be there. Helen continued, "Sister Isidore in charge of the old ladies said we can visit them after dinner. Then we can visit the old men this evening after Benediction."

We reached the nursery at the top of the middle building where there were rows of white painted iron cots around the wall, some holding tiny sleeping babies. A couple of toddlers were sitting on potties while the rest were in little groups, either being told a story or singing in a ring. We spent a good time in there, joining in with the singing and watching in wonder as one of the exes changed nappies. I couldn't believe babies were so small.

"We were all that tiny once," said Sister Columbanus, who had charge of the Nursery. Was she trying to tell me that nuns were babies once? I couldn't believe that. I remember having a pang of jealousy when Lindy cuddled a toddler who had taken a tumble, and then worrying about getting a black mark on my nice clean soul, because jealousy is a sin.

After dinner, we made our way to the old ladies' department. We were taken in to see the bed-ridden. They were so pleased to see us and some gave us sweets. We sang for them and a few had tears in their eyes. One lady beckoned me to her.

I went to her bedside and she held my hand with one of her gnarled old hands and with the other she gave me an orange. I hadn't seen an orange since last Christmas and couldn't believe my luck. Of course I'd have to share it six ways but what a lovely treat. After reciting poems and dancing, we returned to the children's wing where we joined the juniors in the playground. It would soon be time for Benediction.

I joined in with a skipping game after putting the orange on a window sill. Two girls turned the rope while we skipped in and out singing, "All in together girls, never mind the weather girls. Put your rouge and powder on, tell the boys you won't be long. When I count to twenty, the rope must be empty. Five, ten, fifteen, twenty."

The bell went for Benediction and I ran to collect the precious orange. But I was too late - someone had stolen it!

Benediction over, we six made our way to visit the old men. "Hello Mr. Houlihan, hello Mr. Alexander," we said, as we recognised the gate man and the man who stoked up the furnaces in the boiler room near our playground.

"Here come the pretty maids," said another man, who we learned was Mr. Gibson. Again, we sang and danced for the men and visited the bedridden. Soon it was time to return to the other children because it would be a "high tea" with jelly and cakes! We chattered away excitedly as we made our way towards Timber Passage, relieved to see that Mickey was nowhere in sight. We turned a corner and I bumped straight into Mr. Gibson.

"Oh, hello, Mr. Gibby Gibby," I said. I wasn't meaning to be rude; I think I was trying to be funny.

He glared at me and said, "Now then…"

With that, I heard a hiss and the words, "Get here this minute!" I walked towards the dreaded figure and knew I was in trouble again. "Apologise this instant to Mr. Gibson!"

I turned to Mr. Gibson and said I was very sorry. He just walked away and, with that, I resigned myself to whatever was about to happen.

"I might have known it was you," said Sister Columba. "Well you've lost your privileges now, young madam. Take off those clothes and get changed into your day things, then go and sit at your own table. There'll be no tea party for you."

Oh this is so unfair, I thought, as tears of rage and self-pity filled my eyes. I went to the changing room and changed out of my white dress then entered the refectory and went to my own table. Lots of eyes were on me as girls wondered why I wasn't joining the other five communicants, but nobody dared speak until we were told to. Temper flared up in me and I lashed out at the plate and knife in front of me. They crashed to the floor and I laid my head on my arms and sobbed. A hand came down on my shoulder and I was hauled to my feet.

"You've really showed yourself in your true colours today, haven't you? And for that show of temper you will now receive six of the best." I held my hands out knowing that if I was to dare pull my hands back I would receive an extra strike.

I went to bed that night with so many mixed emotions. I was ashamed because I'd disgraced myself on such a special day, and my soul was probably black as soot again. I had been so happy for most of the day, but to deprive me of my high tea was more than I could bear. Why, oh why was I in this place? I wanted to go and live with Aunt Eva again. At least she loved me. I knew Lindy loved me too but I think even she was ashamed of my behaviour that day.

Chapter 5

"What are you making?" I asked Lindy one day.

We were all in the playroom because it was raining outside. She was sitting in a corner sewing two strips of white cotton. She carried on sewing as she explained, "Winnie has to find two ribbons for her hair by Sunday or she will get the cane, so I've torn two strips of material off one of the tea towels and I'm hemming them all around to make a pair of ribbons for her. You can't tell they've been torn off something but the only thing I'm worried about is the colour. It's a pity I can't dye them. I have no dye."

"What about using some ink," I suggested.

"Oh, you clever little girl. I never thought of that."

On hearing those words, I swelled up with pride... then had a pang of guilt. Pride is a sin!

Our ink came in powder form and had to be mixed up in a jug with cold water every Monday, after which someone would have to go round and fill all the inkwells in our desks.

When Lindy had finished hemming the ribbons, she mixed up some ink and dipped them in. They were then wound round a pipe leading to a radiator and left to dry. The ink stained Lindy's fingers and she had a dickens of a job trying to remove the stains with a scrubbing brush and carbolic soap.

The finished ribbons were given to Winnie just in time for Sunday Mass and she was delighted and so grateful to my sister. Lindy was pleased too in that she had been able to help someone in trouble, but it all backfired on her. She'd forgotten to hem the side of the tea towel where she'd torn off the two strips. Sister wanted to know who was responsible and Lindy had to own up.

"Why did you tear it? Sister wanted to know.

"I cut my finger and used it for a bandage," Lindy lied. If she had told the truth, she would have been in more trouble for stealing the ink and Winnie might have been in trouble too. This way she got only four strokes of the cane and made to sew up the side of the tea towel.

Nothing was allowed to be wasted in the convent. Bolts of calico would be delivered to the linen room and sheets were made from these. When the sheets wore out, they were turned side-to-centre or patched. Once they were past repairing, they would be made into pillow cases or tea towels. From then on, if you were lucky, a bit might be available for you to stitch around and use as a hanky. Every item you possessed had to have your number either written or embroidered on it.

Embroidery and mending was taught in the sewing room run by Sister Methodius and a lady named Frances Farthing. She lived in the old ladies department and had only one leg. Rumours circulated that her leg had been bitten off by a big crocodile but no-one ever asked her if this was true or not, or how exactly she'd lost her leg. You just didn't ask questions like that: it was considered rude.

We would see her every weekday, hobbling along Timber Passage on her crutches at 8.50 am to take up her place in the sewing room with Sister Methodius. She would patch our clothes and make dresses, nightdresses and pinafores using a treadle sewing machine. We thought she was marvellous; it was hard enough to use a treadle machine with two legs, let alone one!

One good thing about lessons in the sewing room was that there was a wireless in there. We'd listen to 'Music While You Work' and 'Mrs. Dale's Diary' while we were taught to knit, sew, darn and embroider. Sister would walk around and inspect what you were doing. If you were stitching a hem, all the stitches had to be small and the same distance apart. Sister had a silver thimble on the middle finger of her right hand and if she was displeased with your work, this thimble would come down on your head four or five times. Not only was this painful but you had to watch as your stitches were ripped out and you had to start again. It was so frustrating, and you weren't allowed to speak unless it was to answer a question from Sister or Frances.

Once you had learnt to sew, you were given a square of worn out sheeting which you doubled over then stitched around it with a loop in the top. Next you would embroider the square with red cotton and cross stitch. You ended up with a one and a half inch square with the embroidered:

+
JMJ
CC
17

The JMJ stood for Jesus, Mary and Joseph. CC stated to the laundry that the garment came from the children's department. The whole thing was then attached to the loop that every garment had sewn into it.

We were very often called by our surnames or our numbers, hardly ever by our Christian names. I do remember being praised once by Frances. She had given me a pinafore to mend. It had a long tear in it and Frances showed me how to mend it without puckering. I took my time with it and then took it to Frances for her inspection. I was pleasantly surprised by her reaction. She showed it to Sister who then showed it to the class saying, "This is how a good darn should look when it is finished, with small neat and tidy stitches."

I swelled with pride, then a little voice in my head said, "Don't be so proud of yourself. Pride is a sin!"

One day, one of the nuns died. She was very old and had been ill for a while. We didn't know her personally, just her name and that she walked hunched up because she had a hump on her back. As was the custom when anyone died in the convent, the passing bell was rung and all would have to kneel down to say the 'De Profundis'. This was a prayer to help the soul of the dead speed off to God.

The nuns had their own cemetery in the grounds of the convent. This was situated at one end of our playground, through a grotto laid out in honour of Saint Bernadette and Our Lady of Lourdes. The cemetery was surrounded by yew trees and was strictly out of bounds.

As was the custom, the dead nun was laid out in her coffin in the chapel surrounded by six long black candles in large brass candlesticks. We were all lined up to pass by the coffin and pay our last respects. Most of us had never seen a dead person before and we were scared. I closed my eyes as we filed past; so did a lot of other girls. We were all pulled out of line and made to go past again, this time with our eyes open. I looked and was amazed at what I saw. She lay there serenely in her black habit as if she was asleep and there was no sign of crookedness - her hump had vanished.

A long Requiem Mass was said and the nun was laid to rest in the little cemetery. A few children had nightmares fearing her ghost would come and haunt them. There were a lot of bed-wetting incidents - including me!

Winter arrived and we were fitted out with jumpers and coats, all of them hand-me-downs. As you outgrew anything, it was passed on to a smaller child. I remember getting so upset and crying when I saw another little girl wearing the blue coat that I had arrived in. Sister shouted at me and told me I was being very selfish; a good Catholic girl shares all of her possessions. I found this very hard to accept. I even had to share Conker, my doll, with another girl who didn't have one. I never played much with Conker after that, especially as the other girl changed her name.

"Conker is a silly name," she said. "I'm going to call her Milly."

"No! Her name is Conker!"

"Milly!"

"Conker!"

"Milly!"

Our voices were getting higher and louder. I wanted to launch myself at her to scratch her eyes out, to pull her hair, to box her ears and, just for good measure, I wanted to kick her backside! But Sister was looking in our direction and fighting and losing your temper is a sin, so I walked away and picked up a book to read. It was snatched away from me and another girl glared at me.

"That's mine!" she said.

"Yes, but we have to share," I said.

"Well you're not sharing this book - it's my own!"

Chapter 6

During 1948, a little girl named Beatrice came to the convent. She was 5 years old and, soon after arriving, all of her hair fell out with stress. She would go to the pharmacy each week to see Sister Teresa who had some sort of medical knowledge. Sister Teresa had no teeth, hence her nickname 'Gummy'. She would smother Beatrice's head with Vaseline, wrap newspaper around it and then put on a cotton bonnet.

Beatrice was told that she could have a sweet if she had one new hair growing when she was unwrapped. Eventually her hair did grow back but it took a long time. A lot of younger children believed she was a German Princess because part of her surname had the word 'castle' in it.

In 1949, Sister Columba left for another convent. Sister Magdalen took over the seniors while a new nun, Sister Mary of Nazareth, had charge of the juniors.

I moved up to Miss Cox's class. Her nickname was Crab, due to us being on the beach one day and a little girl excitedly saying, "Oh look, Miss Crab. There's a Cox!" - and so the name stuck.

I liked her a lot although she would use the edge of a ruler on your knuckles if she was displeased with you.

I believe she joined to become a nun but could not cope with the rules of the religion; instead, she stayed on to help with teaching. She was a self-taught pianist and just loved cats. She also loved geraniums and put pots of them on the refectory tables to cheer the place up.

There was a small bookcase in her classroom and I delighted losing myself in reading Grimm's Fairy Tales, Aesop's Fables and Hans Christian Anderson.

I felt I was growing up a little because we went from using a slate and slate pencil to a real note book and proper pencil to do our work.

In our playroom, situated on the ground floor, there was a stage where twice a year we would perform concerts for the nuns and old people: one at Christmas and one on Reverend Mother Superior's Feast Day.

Miss Cox's class. I'm mostly hidden on the right, behind the girl with the bow in her hair.

Weeks before each we would be learning dances, songs and poems, plus sketches and plays. We would really look forward to the big day, especially as we were allowed to curl our hair the night before. This would be done by winding our hair round strips of rags. It was absolute agony to sleep in.

We were encouraged to paint pictures for the front of programmes and write a list of events inside. Only the best were chosen to be used and given to the nuns. The best one of all was handed to Mother Superior and it was considered a great privilege to have your picture chosen. I never had any of my pictures deemed good enough for this. I remember having to stay behind in the classroom one day to finish off one of my paintings. I managed to upset the jar or water I was using and I went to the changing room to refill it, but found the door was locked so I promptly finished off my 'masterpiece' in spit!

I usually had good parts given to me to play on stage, although I was nearly always playing the part of a villain. In one nativity play I was the innkeeper and my 'daughter' had just told Mary and Joseph they could use the stable. I reprimanded the girl (her name was Haven) and got so wrapped up in the part that I slapped her really hard around her face. I heard the audience gasp and poor Haven had a red mark on her face afterwards. We learned lots of Irish songs as most of the nuns were Irish. We also did Irish and Scottish dancing as well as reciting poems and I still remember a lot of those poems, even now.

That Christmas I received a parcel from my new mother which contained a lovely brush and comb. It was a gorgeous pink colour and had the word 'Addis' printed on it. I put it in my cubby hole in the washroom.

Our washroom was on the second floor, across a red tiled passage from the two dormitories. On one wall was a row of mirrors, child height, and along another stood twelve wash basins. Yet another wall had three footbaths and in the centre of the room stood two rows of cubby holes, numbered 1 to 80. Under each cubby hole was a hook for hanging your flannel and towel. In the cubby hole was your brush and comb plus a toothbrush and mug.

Dentfrice toothpaste.

Toothpaste came in a round tin: it was called Gibbs Dentifrice. One tin had to last a month and both seniors and juniors would have to share this tin. It always ran out long before the month was up.

The soap came in foot-long bars which were then cut into twelve 1" bars. It was red carbolic soap and you could often see where mice had been nibbling at it.

On leaving the washroom, to the left was a large statue of Saint Joseph which stood on a small cupboard. This cupboard, we were told, was strictly out of bounds unless you were a teenager. We often wondered what it contained but were too scared to look inside in case a senior saw you and would give you a clip round the ears for being nosey.

Clean knickers were issued once a fortnight and when it was time to change them, we would have to line up to show the crutch to sister before putting them into the laundry bag. Toilet paper was almost non-existent, so lots of us had skid marks in our knickers.

One nun, Sister Leonard, who I believe was Scottish would say, "Line up and show your brix and let's hope there is no cement in them!" I never knew what she meant for ages after. We soon learned that if we wore them inside out, we could show her a fairly clean pair.

One week after clean knickers, we were issued a clean chemise, a horrid starched thing that served as a vest. A lot of us would stuff them under our mattresses instead of wearing them. Nightdresses changed every month, when sheets were changed.

We washed our hair every Saturday morning with carbolic soap then we'd walk towards a tin bath full of warm water containing a solution of Jeyes Fluid. Sometimes too much Jeyes was put in and we would walk away with streaming and stinging eyes. The Jeyes was supposed to keep nits away. It didn't always work. Occasionally we would have an outbreak and our hair would be plastered with paraffin and raked with a nit comb.

Chapter 7

Pope Pius XII declared that 1950 was to be a "Jubilaeum Maximum". All "faithful" were invited to Rome to "celebrate a Holy Year", to "respect the commandments of Christ" and "to change and sanctify one's life". Obviously, we could not travel to Rome so we were given badges and pictures: it seemed every week or so there was something going on to do with religion.

Most schools taught the three 'R's'. Ours were the four 'R's' - 'reading, 'riting, 'rithmetic and religion'. Aside from the regular daily Mass, rosary and Benediction, because it was Holy Year we had three day retreats, holy hour, forty hour expositions... and I almost dreaded when Lent came around.

A few days before Ash Wednesday, all the palms that were hanging on our bed heads were taken away to be burned. These ashes were used during the Ash Wednesday Mass, where we would all line up in front of the priest. He would put his thumb into the ashes and make a cross on our foreheads while saying in Latin,

"Remember, man, that thou art dust and unto dust thou shalt return."

We were told that the longer we kept the ashes on our foreheads, the more souls would be released from Purgatory. I can't remember who told us this, but we believed it. It we thought the ash was wearing off, some of us would scamper up to the big coal pile near the laundry and blacken our foreheads with a cross again.

Lent was a very morbid time throughout the convent. All the statues in the church were covered in purple material. We were all encouraged to give up something for Lent. Most of us said we would give up sweets. This wasn't exactly hard for us as sweets were still on ration and we seldom saw them.

Some girls did have sweets sent to them and they did try to keep them until Easter but they would have to hide them or they might find one or two missing. I'm ashamed to admit that I did thieve once or twice.

During Lent we did our yearly spring-cleaning. The children did all the work, washing down all the walls. Tables and chairs were taken outside and scrubbed with very hot water and soda.

All the parquet floors in the refectory, school room and playroom were scattered with damp tea leaves before being thoroughly swept and then scrubbed back to white wood. When dry, two girls would get on their knees and apply wax polish (called Ronuk, I think) which was mixed with paraffin while the rest of us would line up with old blanket squares on out feet and, to the tune of "We'll make the keel row" we would sing, "P.O.L.I.S.H." and polish with our feet in time to the song. The floors absolutely gleamed. Bathrooms, washrooms, lavatories, passages and stairs were scrubbed every week.

On every landing there was a broom cupboard. These housed all the cleaning tools but everything had to be put in just so. Brooms had to have all the fluff cleaned off before being hung up with the dustpans and hand brushes; buckets were scrubbed clean; scrubbing brushes stored 'bristles up'; floor cloths draped over buckets to dry; kneeling pads were stacked neatly by the folded dusters and polishing cloths that had been made from the worn out blankets.

When our blankets came back from the laundry after the yearly wash, they were thoroughly examined. Worn out ones were put aside and used to patch those not so worn. If they were too far gone, they would be cut into squares and used for foot polishers: two squares would be stitched together with proper blanket stitching and then your number would be embroidered in the corner. Lord help anyone who was caught using someone else's square - they were personal squares, made and embroidered by you. There were a couple of long handled bumpers that could be used for buffing up the floors but most of us liked to use our own squares.

All the cleaning had to be done by Holy Week. On Good Frida, we were expected to not speak from 12 noon until 3.00 pm. This was supposed to be the length of time that Jesus hung on the cross before dying and we were told to try to focus on the suffering he endured during that time.

Holy Saturday was a day of anticipation for the coming Easter festivities. There was no morning Mass and all the statues were unveiled. The Priest visited every wing in the convent to bless all the rooms with Holy Water.

Our bright, clean dormitory was gleaming and shining with new counterpanes on the beds, and all was spick and span for the blessing; and the new palms that had been given to us on the previous Palm Sunday were fastened to our bed heads.

On Easter Sunday, we went to morning Mass. The chapel was filled with yellow and white flowers and lit candles were placed all over the altar in shining brass candlesticks. It was a solemn Mass, spoken and sung in Latin. The church was packed full of people, some resident, some from outside.

I enjoyed religious festivities like this; the smell of incense, candles and flowers, plus the singing, always stirred something inside me.

After, there was always a good breakfast made all the better because we were allowed to speak during the meal. The rest of the day we could spend amusing ourselves.

At Whitsuntide we were invited to the annual Horse Show at The Polegrove, a local recreation ground.

The people of Bexhill were very kind to us. Every Christmas we would be invited to see the pantomime at the De La Warr Pavilion. We would be offered occasional visits to the local cinema, The Ritz, to see various films and the children from the nearby Downs School would donate toys to put on a huge Christmas tree. Yes, amongst all the hardship there WERE happy times spent there.

I believe I was Confirmed that year in Saint Mary Magdalen's Church in town. I wanted my confirmation name to be Lindy but was told there was not a Saint by that name so I had to choose another: I chose Veronica.

In August we gave a concert for the nuns and old people. We sang, danced and recited poems. Our play was entitled The Message of Fatima. It was about three little children in Portugal - Jacinta, Francisco and Lucia - who regularly saw visions of the Virgin Mary. I played the part of Francisco. I just loved to act.

Lindy had moved up to the exes some time ago and I joined the seniors. I was given a new number - 17 - Lindy's old number. I was highly delighted.

Lindy now worked in the nursery with Sister Mary Clare, a very kind nun who had replaced Sister Columbanus. Lindy enjoyed working with her and when she got her first pay (ten shillings, I believe) she went straight to town and bought me a new pair of blue ankle socks. How I loved that beautiful, loving and generous girl.

Because I was now a senior, I was given work to do. My first job was to join five other girls and go to clean the church which was run by Sister Carthage (nicknamed Pigeon because she walked pigeon toed).

Floors and benches were mopped and dusted daily. During services, the children knelt on one side of the church with the old residents and outsiders, on the other side. We never had kneeling pads but all the other benches had them and these had to be brushed and rolled up daily. I hated doing one particular bench where an old man would kneel: he would cough and spit all over the kneeler and it was not a nice job clearing that up!

The nuns had their own private chapel which was curtained off from us. We did not clean that area as we were not allowed to go the other side of the altar rails and so this was done by Sister herself. The floor around the altar was black and white marble and Sister used an electric polisher for that.

All the life size statues were dusted and the brass and silver candlesticks had to be cleaned in the sacristy, next door to the altar. Sister Carthage would see to the priest's vestments and altar cloths, then appoint a couple of girls to clean the candle grease from the candlesticks.

I remember Pauline opening a cupboard and finding a box of hosts, the round wafers used for communion. She took a handful and shared them out, stating that it was ok because they had not been blessed by the priest yet. She got a good beating when it was discovered that the box had been opened and she was told she would go to hell.

Chapter 8

We would spend about six months before in each job before being sent to others and eventually I was sent to the laundry to work. The laundry was run by Sister Isidore (I can't remember her nickname, but I know she had one). She ran the laundry as well as the old ladies' department. Lots of the exes would be working in there and all the washing had to be done on a Monday.

The sheets and pillowcases, etc., were boiled in a huge copper. I loved the smell of boiling washing. It was then rinsed and put into a great big spin dryer which terrified me. All was then pegged out in the drying grounds near the chicken run. The rest was usually washed in large hand basins with white soap.

If the weather turned wet, it was a mad dash to bring the washing in and hang it on heated pipes that were pulled out from the wall.

The nuns' clothes were washed separately by a trusted ex girl and were not seen by us. There was always a whispered question from Sister: "Have you been to Saint Joseph's cupboard?" I often puzzled over what that was all about but if I asked the ex I was told to mind my own business.

I remember Ann told me she once looked inside the cupboard and quickly shut it again. I asked what she saw in there and she said it was full of bandages which were all bloody and she thought they were left over from the soldiers who were injured during the war.

On Tuesdays it was back to the laundry for the ironing. In the ironing room there stood a huge calender, an ironing machine which took care of the large items like sheets, pillow cases, towels and counterpanes, etc. Two girls would feed the items in on one side while two girls would extract them from the other side, folding the items before putting them into wicker baskets.

There were large tables covered with padding and two electric irons, used only by the exes. A large black coke-heated stove had sections on top where flat irons were heated before being used on other stuff. I can remember girls spitting on the irons to see if they were hot enough to use.

A lot of nuns' habits had to be starched, so this was another thing we were taught to do.

My next job was to help out in the kitchen. Another pair of hands was needed because a "Child of Mary" convention was coming and tea and cakes were being provided. I had never actually been inside the kitchen before and it looked enormous, with high ceilings that had glass in the roof. The kitchen stood in the centre of the convent and had lots of sinks and ovens. Six hatches were in various walls, pointing to all the different departments. Each hatch had a sliding panel through which food was passed at specified times and in a specific order: babies, children, exes, old men, old ladies and nuns.

I walked into the place with my eyes all agog, to be met by Sister Augustine (nicknamed S'gusting - our way of saying disgusting).

"Yes girl?" she greeted me.

"I've come to help."

"Good. Take this and beat it thoroughly."

She put a large bowl in my hand with some sort of mixture in it and a wooden spoon. I started to stir it whilst looking about at all the activity going on.

Sister came bustling past me and said, "For heaven's sake, girl! I said beat it. Come on, put some vim into it."

I duly picked up the cylinder of Vim by one of the sinks and innocently asked her, "How much?"

She grabbed the bowl from me, shouting, "Out of my sight, you stupid girl. Ask them to send someone with an ounce of sense."

I really didn't know what I had done to make her so cross with me. I never worked in the kitchen again.

My next stint was learning to clean out lavatories. Josephine, an ex, was to show me how. Sister said Josephine's toilets were so clean you could eat out of them and, when I had finished cleaning, mine were to be the same. So, armed with bucket, scrubbing brush, Vim, a large cloth and Jeyes Fluid plus a knife with a broken tip, we set off for the six lavatories.

First, you would kneel down in front of the lavatory and put the large cloth into the bowl, swishing it back and forth until all the water disappeared. Next, you took your knife with the broken tip and chipped away at the limescale that had built up around the bowl. Finally, you gave a good sprinkling of Vim inside and outside the bowl and scrubbed the wooden seat that was fixed to the rim.

Once that was completed you would start on the white tiled walls. As I have already said, toilet paper was almost non-existent so the walls were usually smeared with unmentionable stuff! You scrubbed the red quarry-tiled floor with carbolic soap and Jeyes Fluid and… job done!

I passed the test and so that was my job for the next six months of my life.

Chapter 9

Reading back on this, it makes it look as if as seniors were working all the time but this was not so. We still had schooling and play times.

We'd play at skipping, hopscotch and statues and we'd also make up completely new games. A favourite of mine was called 'Cobbler'.

One girl would face a window sill and hold onto it while putting one leg behind her for another girl to hold. She would then hop and cross the other leg over the one being held and we would all chant, "Cobbler, cobbler mend my shoe, have it done by half past two. Half past two will be too late, have it done by half past eight, eight, eight, eight." You would keep on hopping and crossing legs until you were exhausted and then it was the next girl's turn.

Another game: playing with two balls thrown against the wall while chanting, "Plainsy, clapsy, round the world and backsy. Touch your heel, touch your toe, touch your knee and under you go."

We'd play long jump and high jump, find pebbles and play five-stones or use a strand of wool to play cats-cradle. In summer we were allowed to go into the field and enjoy ourselves on the swings and see-saw.

We'd love to eat the sorrel, vetch and hawthorn leaves and berries. Queenie once climbed the oak tree and came down with some acorns. Some of us tried to eat them - yuk!

There were lovely red berries on the yew trees around the nuns' cemetery. Mary said, "Don't eat them they're poisonous."

But Ann said, "I tried one and it was very sweet. I didn't chew it, just swallowed." So we had one each. Then there were little black berries on the privet hedge to try.

That evening a lot of us got sick, so it was decided every child would be given a dose of Epsom salts in warm water. We all stood around the walls of the refectory and had to stay there until we had drunk it all. It was foul!

It so happened that I was standing by one of the radiators so when Miss Cox's back was turned I poured mine behind it. Others saw me and did the same. Some ended up in Miss Cox's geraniums on the table.

Next day, we saw the odd job man checking the radiators for leaks!

Chapter 10

Lindy came to me one day and I knew by the look on her face that she was going to tell me something bad. She put her arms around me and said she would be leaving to go to another Nazareth House in East Finchley to train as a child nurse.

"Am I coming with you?"

"No my darling, you must stay here."

"No! No you can't leave me here!"

I burst into tears. She held me closer and I begged and pleaded with her to let me go with her.

"I'm not going straight away, I will be here a little while longer."

I couldn't let go of her. My arms were around her waist and she cradled me against her. I could feel her heart beating in my ear. I just couldn't stop crying and felt as if I wanted to crawl inside of her so we wouldn't ever be parted.

"Don't go, PLEASE don't go!" I pleaded. My heart was breaking.

Sister came past and wanted to know what was going on. A girl told her the reason. Sister told me I should not be making such a fuss and that I was being selfish for making my sister feel so bad.

"Pull yourself together and get yourself ready for Benediction," she said.

Lindy peeled herself away from me and gave me a kiss, then left to go back to her job in the Nursery. In a daze, I put on the green crocheted beret we all wore in church and stood in line with the other girls before walking along Timber Passage to the chapel. I was broken hearted, hurt and angry. I failed to understand why I was labelled as being selfish.

The rest of the day passed in a haze. Lindy came to my bed that night. I was still crying and had a pounding headache. She told me that wherever she was she would always love me and be thinking of me. Again I pleaded with her to take me with her and told her I would never, ever be naughty again. She burst into tears and said she wasn't punishing me by going away, but it was time for her to go out to work and she needed to train as a child nurse so she could get a job. We both hugged and cried. Eventually she tucked me in, gave me another kiss and left.

I fell into a fitful sleep and when I woke I thought it had all been a bad dream. I followed the usual morning routine and when in church for morning Mass, I looked around for my sister but could not see her. I looked for her again when doing my morning chores after breakfast. I couldn't concentrate on my school work and waited to see if she would come by at dinnertime. There was no sign of her - where could she be? Surely that bad dream I had last night couldn't be true!

I eventually sneaked up to the top floor to the nursery to see what could have happened to her. Sister Mary Clare told me that Lindy had left that morning for her new job in East Finchley.

"GONE?? But she didn't even say goodbye!" I wailed.

I just sank to the floor and sobbed my heart out. Life was so unfair. My mother didn't want me.

My father wanted his own life without the bother of me. My brother was separated from me. My Aunt Eva was not allowed to have me. And now my beloved Lindy had deserted me.

What had I done to deserve this? Was I so bad that nobody wanted me? I began to wonder why I had been born. What use was I on this Earth, if nobody wanted me? How was I going to live without the one person left in my life who truly loved me? My lovely sister was gone. I might just as well be dead.

I decided I would hold my breath to make myself die, but I just got very dizzy and ended up gasping. Then a voice in my head told me, "That's the same as suicide and it's a mortal sin. You will go straight to hell."

My tears just would not stop. Something died inside of me then and I swear, to this day I have never been whole again. I was a wreck and broken inside. There was an ache around my heart and a feeling of utter and desperate loneliness. Who was there for me now? Who would give me a hug when needed?

I felt so rejected. Everyone who was connected to me was gone. I walked around in a daze and couldn't stop crying. She didn't even say goodbye.

In bed that night, I prayed to God. I asked if this was a punishment for being naughty. I vowed to him that I would be good for evermore if he would only let my beloved sister come back to me. I couldn't sleep and, in the morning, my eyes were so swollen with crying that I could hardly see out of them. My tears just would not stop.

I was told to pull myself together and to stop snivelling. I was reminded that at least three quarters of the girls there had lost someone in their short lives. How could I put into words what I was feeling? Nobody seemed to know or even care about what I was going through. Had I really been so wicked to deserve this hurt? "Yes," said a voice in my head. "Stop thinking about yourself so much and think of others."

I tried, but the thought of her leaving without even saying goodbye was starting to make me feel even worse. Every time that thought crossed my mind I would start crying again. Eventually I got the name of 'cry-baby' and someone even accused me of crying to get sympathy. "You're just a notice box," was the way of saying it.

This made me angry. I was not crying for sympathy, I was crying because I was hurting inside.

Gradually the teasing eased off - but not the hurting. I managed to hold off my tears until I was on my own, usually in bed at night.

I received a letter from Lindy saying she had settled down in her new home and was happy in her training. (How could she be happy while I was so unhappy?)

It was at this point in my life that I turned to food for comfort and gradually started to get fatter.

Chapter 11

In August it was decided we would swap convents for two weeks. Two coaches arrived from Isleworth in Middlesex with girls in the same age bracket as us, all highly excited because they were going to be by the seaside for two weeks. Many of them had never seen the sea in their lives.

After dinner, it was our turn to board the coaches going back to Isleworth. Excitement filled the air. When we arrived we went straight to the chapel to thank God for our safe journey, then we went exploring the children's wing. Isleworth was run along similar lines to Bexhill, housing a community of nuns and a few elderly residents, but with no nursery for babies. There was a nice big playground with a climbing frame: when I went to get on it, I was told to get off as I was too big and might break it.

There was a large field to play in and a big wall along one side of it, so high that we could not see over it. One area of the field would get very soggy sometimes and we were told that we were close by the river Thames which would overflow and flood parts of the field.

We had quite a few outings that fortnight. We visited Hampton Court Maze, Richmond Park and Madam Tussauds. We even had a boat trip along the river where I spent the whole time counting all the dead fish I saw floating in the water.

All in all, it was a lovely two weeks, although I still felt desperately lonely and would get very moody.

Back in Bexhill again, life went on as usual. I moved up to Sister Magdalen's class (her nickname was Maggot). I joined the choir and just loved learning to sing 'plain chant'. Music took me out of myself somehow and I would stand by the organ in the choir loft and turn the pages of sheet music while Sister played. I couldn't read music properly but I seemed to know when it was time to turn the page.

My father and stepmother came to visit me for my birthday. They said they would take me to Hastings and when we got outside I almost collapsed with surprise. There was a motorbike and side-car. Dad lifted up the lid of the side-car and I got inside. He then climbed on and started up the bike and Mum climbed on behind him. I was absolutely thrilled. A lot of the kids were looking out of the window and I was delighted because I was sure I was the only one there to have parents who owned a motor bike. When we got to Hastings, Dad said I could ride pillion on the way back. I did enjoy that birthday especially as I was given a florin (2/-) when they left me; but the money was soon taken from me when I returned to the convent.

Christmas was approaching and we learned more new songs, dances and poems for the upcoming concert. More pictures were painted for the programmes and we also made booklets in which we wrote down the words to carols and Latin responses for Midnight Mass. On top of that, we made paper decorations for the refectory and playroom and the seniors learned how to make carnations and roses from coloured crepe paper.

About two weeks before Christmas, all parcels that arrived for the children were put in a special room until it was time to give them out on the actual day. I think this was done to make sure every child had a parcel to open. Those children who had no one had parcels made up for them by the nuns. No one was forgotten.

All of our letters and parcels were opened before being given to us. The same with letters we wrote home. They had to be read first before they were posted.

I received a lovely red pencil box from Mum and Dad. It contained a pen and pencil with a rubber and sharpener and a small ruler. I was the envy of other girls who only managed to make their pencil boxes from empty date boxes.

I also received a hand drawn Christmas card from Alec; Lindy sent me a parcel containing a doll and a bar of White Windsor scented soap.

White Windsor soap.

Everyone wanted to try the soap so it didn't last long.

Chapter 12

Bridget and I were called into the classroom one day to be told by Sister that we were to go to Downs School to sit for a scholarship. We were most surprised - what was this all about? Sister said if we passed, we would attend the local Grammar school. What on earth was a Grammar school? Were we to be sent away?

A new girl told us that a Grammar school was a place for posh, snooty people and Bridget and I would not get in there because we weren't posh enough.

When we got to Downs there were lots of other girls from different schools all sitting for the same exam. One girl asked us what school we went to. We said, "Nazareth House."

"Where's that?" she asked.

Another girl said, "Oh, that's where all those poor kids go and get looked after by the nuns."

"Ah! You poor creatures," said the first girl with pity.

We went in and sat for the exam but I remember feeling most uncomfortable among all these strange girls who were probably looking down on us. Anyway, we never passed and I was quite relieved as I didn't want to be classed as posh or snooty. I think Sister was disappointed. She said she was sure one of us would have passed.

At Whitsun, I spent a week away in Brixton with my father and stepmother. They rented a top floor flat in Gresham Road and Mum sent a rail ticket for me to catch the train to Victoria where she would meet me. I used to enjoy her showing me around parts of London. I particularly loved to see the billboards advertising all sorts of things. One I do remember clearly was a giant picture of a large lady on a bike with a basket of clean washing and a packet of powder perched on her handle bars. She had a big grin on her face and an arm outstretched to turn a corner and there was a slogan in large lettering stating 'Turn to Tide for the cleanest wash of all.' I thought that was so clever and amusing.

Brixton Market was another place I would love to visit with my stepmother. We would go there for fresh fruit and vegetables.

I slept on a camp bed in the sitting room and promptly wet the bed on the first night there. I expected a good telling off or to be caned but was pleasantly surprised to be told, "Never mind, accidents happen."

I was always led to understand that stepmothers were wicked. In every story book I had ever read there was nearly always a wicked stepmother but that was clearly not the case here. Although I was a bit in awe of her, she showed she had a caring side.

Next day, Mum told me that Lindy and Alec would be visiting. I was highly delighted and waited in great anticipation. I would get to see my lovely sister and also my big brother again. What a greeting we all had.

A great fuss was made of me and Alec told me he had left school and was now working. His voice had broken and he looked so grown up. Lindy then told me that I would be going back with her to East Finchley later that evening to stay the night there. Apparently, Mum and Dad had to attend an unexpected and urgent meeting the next day and Mum would collect me the next evening.

Alec accompanied Lindy and I to the underground later that day. We parted there as Alec had to catch a train, going in a different direction to where Lindy and I were going. Little did I know at the time that that would be the last time I saw him until we were both grandparents.

Lindy and I carried on to Nazareth House in East Finchley where the nuns made a great fuss of me. What a difference from Bexhill. I was in heaven being with my darling sister again. Next day she showed me all over where she worked with tiny babies. We then explored the garden where I was fascinated to be shown a tree trunk that had turned to stone. No-one seemed to know how old it was.

The day passed too quickly and Mum arrived to take me back to Brixton. Lindy came to the underground station with us. I just couldn't bear this parting again and when I got on to the train I burst into tears. I knew all of the feelings and sorrow I felt when my sister left me the last time would return again. "Will I ever see her again?" I thought as the train pulled away. Mum asked why I was crying but I couldn't put into words just what I was feeling. Would I be told off for snivelling? I stopped crying and tried not to think about the renewed loneliness I knew I was going to feel.

Back in the flat at Brixton, Mum showed me how to make custard for the trifle she was making for dessert, and I laid the table for when Dad got home. He was whistling as he came up the stairs to the top flat. I asked him to show me how to whistle and we had a good giggle at my efforts. After the evening meal we played Monopoly. I wanted to talk about my sister but I knew I would start crying again so just left it and went to bed, feeling so sad.

Next day, I had to return to Bexhill. Before leaving, Mum said my hair needed washing so she mixed up something called Drene Shampoo. It came in powder form and had to be mixed up with cold water. When she had finished I asked her where the Jeyes Fluid was for rinsing my hair. She just did not believe me when I told her that was what we used.

When I got back to school I was told that I had missed seeing Princess Elizabeth being driven through Bexhill on her way to Lewes. All the girls went to the bottom of Penland Road to wave and cheer her on her way.

We went back to Isleworth for two weeks again in the summer. I went to the soggy area of the field by the high wall: I wanted to be alone for a while. I heard a man whistling a tune on the other side of the wall. I convinced myself it was my Dad. Well, we were by the River Thames and I knew that was in London and my Mum and Dad lived in London and I knew my Dad could whistle just like this man...

"Dad!" I shouted. No response.

"Dad! It's me!" Still no response.

"Dad! Dad, its Phyllis!" The whistling went on. Obviously my Dad didn't want to take any notice of me. Rejected again. Why did no one want me? I started to cry.

Just then I heard Clare calling me. "There you are. We were looking for you. We're playing rounders and need another one. Can you come?"

Away I went and enjoyed the game.

Again we enjoyed several outings to places like Kew Gardens, Bushey Park and Hampton Court: we also visited the Mother House at Hammersmith. Some of us went to Battersea Fun Fair where word had got around that we were orphans and so had lots of free rides. We had such a great time we were quite disappointed when it was time to return to Bexhill.

We gave a concert for Reverend Mother's Feast Day; songs and dances as usual, along with a play about St. Joan of Arc that had been written by Miss Cox. I did not have a part in this play because I was acting in the juniors' play called 'The Wrong Side of the Bed.' Little Beatrice played the part of a naughty child who was summonsed to see the Flower Queen because she had run right through a bed of flowers and trampled them. I was the Goblin who had to take the naughty child to see the Flower Queen.

It was a colourful little play with lots of the juniors dressed up as different flowers. All the costumes had been made by Sister Methodius and Frances Farthing: Frances now had an electric attachment fitted to her treadle sewing machine which made things a lot easier for her.

The local dentist would visit us twice a year to examine our teeth. He would make notes as to who needed treatment. His name was Mr. Clare and he had a practice in the town. My name was put down as I was having trouble with bleeding gums. A couple of other kids also needed treatment so the following week we made our way to town to the practice, which was in a big house near the sea front. We marvelled at the lavatory which had roses painted on the porcelain bowl, inside and out.

One thing we liked to do was to write the numbers of our best friends on our arms. I had penned a few numbers on my own arm in ink and, when I got into the dentist's chair, Mr. Clare looked at my arm, gave me a smile and muttered, "Poor child." It was only years after that I realised he must have thought I had been rescued from a prison camp in Germany or something.

Every now and then, a priest named Father Arbuthnott would visit; he would like to see all the girls who had been sent in from the Southwark Catholic Rescue Society. He would ask how we were but I must say I was quite frightened of him because he had a much disfigured face. It turned out that he had gone into a bombed building during the war to rescue a child who was trapped in there. He had been badly burned during the rescue. I never knew the outcome of that story, whether the child survived or not.

Beatrice's mother had a job in the NAAFI and so was able to send Beatrice jars of malt and cod liver oil. These would be locked in a cupboard and dished out to her every so often. I wanted to know what it tasted like so I found a way to pick the lock and steal a dessert spoonful every so often. I left the cod liver oil well alone as it tasted YUK! The greengage jam and sugar were kept in the same cupboard, so a spoonful of each would go into my mouth as well as the malt.

One girl had a small birthday cake sent to her and, after she'd had a slice, this was also locked away. Again I picked the lock and helped myself to a slice. I was just about to have a bite when I heard someone coming. I threw the cake into a jug on the window sill and made my escape. When I returned to eat my ill-gotten gains I found I had tossed the cake into a jug of Jeyes Fluid!

I knew all this stealing was a sin but I didn't care anymore. God hadn't helped me when my sister left, so why should I be good anymore? I still went to confession but simply reeled off the same old sins each time.

On another trip to raid the cupboard I was caught red-handed by Miss Cox and reported to Sister Magdalen. She gave me the cane and locked me in the classroom. I was told to kneel down and think about what I had done. I had to stay like that until she returned.

She came back when it was dark and all the children were in bed. I was sure she had forgotten about me and imagined I would spend the night alone. I felt frightened, lonely and desperately unhappy. Where was my Lindy? I needed her reassuring hug and kind words. All I got was a telling off for daring to turn the lights on and wasting electricity. I was sent to bed and reminded to confess my sin of stealing next time I went to confession.

Chapter 13

Ann and I were on our way to collect some used tea leaves from the kitchen for throwing on the playroom floor before it was swept after playtime. We were passing the laundry when we saw an open door to the outhouse which was usually locked. We looked inside and saw a jumble of odds and ends. Among this lot I saw an old handbag and when I looked inside I found a florin (2/-). We whooped for joy and decided we would sneak out later to buy some goodies and then have a 'midnight feast'.

Later, we decided Ann would be the one to go as she was always missing when our numbers were called to see if we were all present. She ran all the way to the Old Town to a little shop called 'The Bee Hive' where she bought a bottle of lemonade, two packets of crisps and a packet of biscuits. We had our 'feast' in the lavatories that night and what a treat that was. One girl who saw us said that, "If you eat in the lavatory you are feeding the devil." Who cared? We didn't.

A lot of things used to be donated to the convent. Things like books, toys and jigsaws, etc., would be given to the children; and so it was with great excitement that, one day, we found a beautiful large rocking horse in our playroom. Nearly everyone lined up to have a go.

Sister Leonard was watching over us at the time and she said we must not sit astride the horse, we must ride it side saddle. When we asked why, we were told that the Royal Princesses always rode side saddle as it was considered very lady-like to do so - and also there was a chance we might tear our knickers!

I didn't bother to line up to have a go. I'd be bound to be told that I would be too big to go on it and might break it. Instead I made a beeline to the piano - I'd try to thump out a tune even though half the notes didn't work.

Next to the playroom was a room we called the 'Green Room'. This was set aside for girls who were in their teens; they had a decent piano in there, plus a bookcase with books and jigsaws, along with a few easy chairs and a table on which was a wind up gramophone with a large stack of records. I couldn't wait to be a teenager.

Madeleine, a senior girl, called me over one day. "Go get Haven. I have to teach you both how to do the Highland Fling for the next concert."

We were both delighted to be chosen. Haven was a very pretty girl with different coloured eyes and we both learned the dance very quickly. Madeleine was a good teacher and made it easy for us by saying, "Side, back, front, kick, toe, heel, toe, kick." All three of us soon had the dance learned to perfection and eagerly looked forward to the concert.

It turned out that Haven had never been baptised. Shock! Horror!

It was arranged that she be baptised in our own chapel by Father Holland. We all attended the baptism and, by the look on her face, I think Haven was a bit embarrassed by it all. Still, she was now without original sin and was, at last, a Catholic like all the rest of us.

We were always encouraged to do kind things for others so we were given a large box of beads to make necklaces, bracelets and brooches for Saint Mary Magdalen's Church Fete. A couple of girls were making rugs and some were embroidering tray cloths and hankies: knitted dishcloths were popular things to make too.

I had somehow managed to get hold of a skein of wool and thought I would make a large pom-pom to hang in a baby's pram. One of the round Gibbs Toothpaste tins had been emptied so I grabbed it to trace round it and use this as the template for my pom-pom.

"Can I have that tin when you've finished with it?" asked Pat.

"Yes, what are you making then?" I asked.

"Nothing," she said. "I've just come in from the playground and it's very dark and cold out there and there is a poor little hedgehog on the step and I want to give it a drink of milk, but I cannot find anything to put the milk in."

I gladly let her have the tin and hoped the hedgehog would survive the night. Next morning I asked if it had drunk the milk.

"No," she said, "it's still there next to the scrubbing brush that I thought was a hedgehog!" How we both laughed at that!

Preparations were being made for the coming Christmas: the usual choir practice for singing at Midnight Mass plus learning new songs and poems for the concert. A few seniors were allowed to collect holly and ivy; the ivy was tied to a long rope which was then draped in loops around the playroom walls and then bunches of wisteria made from paper were hung between the loops, all finished off with strands of silver lametta. More flowers in the form of paper carnations and roses were made for the refectory and everywhere looked wonderful.

A couple of days before Christmas, the school choir assembled in Timber Passage and we sang 'Here we come a'wassailing' as we made our way to sing carols to the old and bedridden. I remembered singing by an old man's bed and watched a tear slide down his face onto his pillow. I was worried in case I got told off for making him cry.

Christmas came and we enjoyed a happy blur of visits to the cinema and to the De La Warr Pavilion for the pantomime. There was also the anticipation of seeing what was in our stockings, which were hung over a rope stretched across the playroom, and the gifts hung on the enormous Christmas tree donated by the children of the Downs School. The Mayor and his wife handed out the parcels and cards that had been stowed away for the past couple of weeks. I loved Christmas, made all the better this year because I was going home for a week in the New Year.

I was collected and driven to Brixton on Dad's motor bike. I had a lovely box of paints as my present and as a surprise we all went to Olympia to see Bertram Mills Circus.

Back at school I bragged about the good time I'd had and all the lovely food that I had to eat but I never let anyone know that I was so sad because I had not heard from Lindy. I supposed she had found a job and forgotten about me. How hurt I was to think that.

That February we heard that King George VI had died. The school choir was assembled together to learn the tune and words to 'Dies Irae', a Latin hymn sung at a Requiem Mass for the dead. There was a very solemn air all about the whole of the convent. We listened to the Proclamation of Queen Elizabeth II on the wireless and the following week we heard the BBC commentary of the funeral procession: all very sombre.

Sister Mary of Nazareth left us and was replaced by Sister Agnes, taking over the care of the juniors. We all missed Sister Mary as she was a very kind nun.

I stayed in Sister Magdalen Ita's class. It seems the older I got, the more I felt she didn't like me. I didn't seem to be able to do anything right. She used a walking stick to cane us with and would lose control at times. I wasn't the only one she seemed to have a 'down' on and a lot of us would show off our bruises after a beating.

Looking back, it must have been very frustrating for her to teach all subjects to a class of about 30 girls, ages ranging from 10 to 14. She was a good teacher and I quite enjoyed the lessons. I loved history and English but it would have been nice to receive a word of praise or encouragement once in a while. I so wanted to be liked and would make up stories to make my classmates laugh at inappropriate times. This would infuriate Sister and so I was at the wrong end of the cane a lot.

I went through a stage of breaking out with boils over the next few months. I would have to visit 'Gummy' in the pharmacy where she would apply a very hot kaolin poultice to the boils. My stepmother wrote to Sister and asked if I was getting the right amount of greens to eat. Sister was not best pleased and I was subjected to remarks such as, "If your mother was that concerned about your health, why doesn't she look after you instead of dumping you on us?" You can imagine how I felt listening to that.

Soon after I had a boil under my right arm and I was determined not to make a fuss about it, so never said anything at all. It gradually got larger and was so painful I would cry when I tried lifting my arm. It turned into an abscess and I had to go to hospital to have it lanced.

From then on I started getting bad stomach pains and one day found I had blood in my knickers. What on earth had I done to cause this? I hadn't climbed over any fences but I had tried to do the splits the other day - was that the cause? The pains were getting worse and Mary asked me if I was alright because I was 'white as a sheet". I told her I was bleeding down below.

"Oh you've got your friends," she said.

"Got what?" I asked.

"Your friends. You get them when you near your teens and it goes on until you are in your forties. You have to see Sister and she will give you some ST's."

I went to see Sister, horrified to think I was going to carry on bleeding until I was in my forties. "I've got my friends," I said to Sister.

"Ah, I guessed that was the reason you were looking so pale. They are called periods, not friends."

She handed me a homemade belt made out of worn out sheeting with two strings in front and two on the back, plus six homemade sanitary towels, made from old sheeting (about four layers stitched together). There were two loops front and back for the strings to do it up. She informed me that I must change it once a day and put the soiled ones into the large bucket of water which was in St. Joseph's cupboard. Aaah! The secret of St. Joseph's cupboard was revealed to me after all this time.

The soiled ones were taken to the laundry every Monday to be boiled and used again. I was so confused and wondered how six towels were going to last until I was in my forties!

That first period lasted nine days and my six towels soon ran out. When I asked for more I was told I could have two more and next time I was to make the six last. I was so relieved when I stopped bleeding. I was told it would come again every four weeks and was not continuous.

When it was bath time, you would have to wait until everyone else had bathed before it was your turn: we all used the same bath water!

Chapter 14

That Easter, the choir was highly praised for their singing at Mass. A huge chocolate Easter egg had been donated to the children and everyone in the choir received a large portion, while the smaller pieces were shared among the rest.

On Easter Monday we spent time on the beach. It was too cold to venture into the sea so we had a lot of fun climbing over the rocks or on the cliffs at Glyne Gap. Later that week we were invited to the Playhouse Cinema to see a film about Robin Hood. We were told that the girl who played the part of Maid Marion was called Joan Rice, who had been brought up in Nazareth House, Nottingham.

Every Sunday in the month of May, we would wear blue dresses and white veils and, if the weather was fine, we would parade around the convent grounds with a large statue of the Virgin Mary. This was carried on a platform and decorated with blue and white flowers and we would sing hymns to Mary all the way round. Part of the way took us past the front of the convent, under the two horse chestnut trees which were in bloom, parallel to the main road.

Across the road was a private girls' school, Ancaster House. Miss Cox would remind us that these girls were daughters of 'the highest in the land' and we should not show ourselves up in front of them by misbehaving.

On the feast of Corpus Christi, we would be dressed in white dresses and veils with a red head band and we would walk to Saint Mary Magdalen's Church in the town to join a huge procession through the streets, ending up with an outdoor benediction. I liked these processions, especially when I was chosen to carry one of the religious banners.

If I remember rightly, one day we all went to some place called The Pilot Field which, I think, was in Hastings. There was a huge crowd there and a Father Patrick Payton preached about the rosary. On the way out I remember some people handing out leaflets and some said abusive things to the nuns. The nuns took no notice but I was rather worried about this and sad to realise there were some people who were anti-Catholic.

I had written to Mum and Dad and told them that we would be going to Isleworth again this year and was delighted when they visited and took me out for the day. On returning, Sister told us that Lindy had phoned to ask how I was, to which my stepmother replied, "Nice to know she is still alive."

I thought, "What on earth did that mean?" They talked a bit more to Sister, then said goodbye and left.

My heart leapt. Lindy had phoned: did that mean she would be coming to see me? It did! She turned up the next day and took me out for a while. She had taken some hours off work to visit me but would have to leave early to return to East Finchley. She told me she had just got engaged and showed me a lovely sparkling ring on her finger. I didn't even know what being engaged meant. She explained she had met a lovely boy named Jack who had asked her to marry him and, because she loved him very much, she had said yes.

Lindy, pictured here eight weeks before her wedding day.

Oh no! My sister now loved someone else. How that hurt me. I was feeling very jealous and I wanted to ask if she loved him better than me, but Sister came in. She and Lindy spoke for a while then Lindy had to dash off. With a quick hug and kiss, she gave me some copies of the comics 'Girls Crystal' and 'School Friend' that she had saved for me. She gave me a lovely smile and a wave and off she hurried. I felt utterly rejected again and didn't like the idea of Lindy loving someone else.

From then on I decided that I was just to accept whatever life threw at me. That way I wouldn't be hurt anymore; mentally hurt, I meant. I carried on as usual: I still made the others laugh when I felt in the mood and accepted the canings and beatings as and when they occurred.

Sister Mary Barbara arrived and replaced Sister Agnes. She had amazing blue eyes and took over looking after the juniors. I liked her very much. Sister Leonard replaced Sister Methodius in the sewing room and taught needlework, darning, embroidery and, under her guidance, I managed to knit a pair of long socks on four knitting needles. I was bragging again to whoever would listen about how clever I was because I learnt how to turn the heel of a sock. Sister Magdalen heard me and told me she would get me a trumpet to broadcast to the world.

We had a new Reverend Mother Superior - Mother Helen. She was very good to us. We had new tables and chairs and a heated cabinet to keep our food hot in the refectory, plus plastic plates, cups and saucers with Nazareth House printed underneath. A new roundabout appeared in our playing field, a bedside cabinet beside each bed and a dozen beds had curtains placed around them for the teenagers. When not in use, these had to be pulled back and pleated in a certain way to keep the dormitory tidy.

That September I became a teenager. [Edit: Phyllis has misremembered this as she reached the age of thirteen in 1952, not 1953.]

I received a lovely brown leather shoulder bag from home and, at last, I was able to join the others in the Green Room. I would make a beeline towards the piano and pick out tunes on there. How I wished we could learn how to play piano.

There was a good selection of books to read. A lot of them were about religion (lives of the saints, etc.) but among them were a good few written by Enid Blyton – 'The Famous Five', 'The Find Outers' and 'Sunny Stories', to name a few. There was always a queue to read these. I remember Eileen telling me to be sure to read 'Shadow, The Sheepdog'. It became a favourite amongst us.

When it was time to visit Saint Mary Magdalen's Church fete again that Christmas, Father Holland told us we could take a little black and white puppy back with us. We promptly named him Shadow.

Miss Cox had a room to herself along the passage and Shadow would stay in there but was always allowed to join us at playtimes. We spent many happy hours with that dog. Ann, the girl who was forced into the classroom to face Bonzo, formed a great attachment to Shadow and would often be found in Miss Cox's room cuddling him.

It was time for us all to have winter coats. Unfortunately, because I had put on quite a bit of weight there was not a coat that would fit me.

There was a store room containing items collected by the nuns who went around begging: that was searched thoroughly but they still couldn't find one that would fasten up around me, so I was taken to the old ladies' department to see if they had anything that would fit me. I ended up with a jacket from a two-piece suit. It was a ghastly maroon colour with huge shoulder pads and a utility label inside. It came down past my knees and was fastened by just one button. I hated wearing it because I was the laughing stock of the whole school.

When it was time to go out for our daily walk I would make any excuse not to go, but it made no difference. I was forced to wear it and join the others. But who was I to make a fuss? Remember; just accept what life throws at you. When I was laughed at, I started to tell them that the suit used to belong to a film star who wore it in a film. I was so relieved they never asked the name of the film star: the only name I could remember was Fatty Arbuckle.

It was another lovely Christmas. That year I received a beautiful sewing set from my Mum and Dad. Mum would write and ask what I would like for Christmas and I would always ask for something 'sensible'. There were times when I'd love to have asked for things like a watch or a camera but I was worried in case they would cost too much. We had no idea of the price of things as we very seldom went out to the shops.

Beatrice received a beautiful pair of roller skates from her Mum. We were all envious but she was very generous and would let us borrow them.

We didn't have much that we could give each other as gifts: only very occasionally did we get pocket money. 6d if you were six years old, 7d if you were seven, and so on. Sister kept a little black notebook in her pocket: if you did something wrong, a mark would be put against your number and you would lose a penny off your pocket money for each mark. Sometimes I would end up owing money (but it was never paid).

On the odd occasion someone did have money, a box would be brought out full of holy pictures which we could buy for a penny each. We would put them in our prayer books.

Very, very occasionally we would be escorted to the town to visit Woolworths where, if anyone was rich enough, you could buy a slide to put in your hair for the princely sum of 6d.

Chapter 15

Girls would be arriving and leaving the convent all the time: girls of all ages and sizes. I didn't like to make too many friends because I felt that if I got too friendly, they would soon be gone like everyone else in my life. However, I did get very friendly with a girl named Pearl who had a little sister called Julie. We would have the odd squabble then make friends again by linking our little fingers together and chanting, "Make up, make up, never do it again, if you do you'll get the cane." Nonsense verses were often used.

During one of our squabbles, I told Pearl I wanted the book I had given her as a present to be returned. She was only halfway through reading it – 'Heidi' - but we had fallen out and I wanted it back. She handed it to me and, with that, a group of girls surrounded me and chanted, "To give a thing and take it back, God will ask you 'Why is that?' If you say you do not know, God will send you down below." I let Pearl have the book back when we made up.

We had a visit from a man from the fire station. He went all over the convent and explained that there should be some changes made. Fire alarms were fitted in every department and a phone was put in the children's wing for us to call the fire station in case of fire.

It was also decided that the babies should be brought down from the top floor and housed on the ground floor where the linen room currently was. The linen room was where all the clean laundry was kept and was run by a lovely sister named Sister Frances Xaviour, assisted by two elderly ladies, Alice and Monica. A few of us were told to help move all the sheets and towels, etc., up to the top floor to where the old nursery had been. Alice and Monica were very grateful for our help, but we enjoyed the task very much.

Soon after, I was told that my next job would be to help out in the linen room. I was delighted and worked very diligently in there. When the clean laundry arrived, my job was to inspect it all and to put aside all the things that needed mending, which would be done by Alice and Monica on their treadle sewing machines. I would then stack everything on shelves that reached from floor to ceiling. Counterpanes, sheets, towels, pillow cases: all and sundry very neatly stacked with the folded edges facing forward. I was praised by all three for my efforts and I swelled with sinful pride.

After a while I was shown how to thread a little hand operated sewing machine and learned to wind thread onto the bobbin. When I had mastered that, I was given a spare bit of sheeting and made myself two handkerchiefs on the little machine; I was even allowed to write my number on them with marking ink. I was so happy and contented working that linen room.

Sister Frances would have her machine in the next room and she would see to all the nuns' habits, making new ones and repairing any that needed it. She would often call me in to thread her machine as her eyesight was getting poor.

On Saturday mornings I would go to clean the linen room and Sister would always bring me a cup of tea with a slice of toast. Oh, what a treat!

Sweets came off ration that year and when Easter arrived there were lots of chocolate eggs shared around.

During daily Mass we would all get in line to go to the altar rails for Holy Communion. The old people would also queue up and there was one old man named Mr. Gully, who had a walking stick. He would carefully put his stick down and then kneel to receive the host. Whoever knelt beside him would help him up and hand him his stick. As we left the chapel, Mr. Gully would hand out sweets and chocolates to a few of the children: such a kind old man. We would all try to be in the right place when he started handing out the goodies.

That Whitsun, I went home for a week. Again, I made my own way to Victoria Station and was met by my stepmother. Before I went to catch the train to Victoria, I was told to wear the hated coat. I bundled it on the rack when I got onto the train and decided I would leave it there on purpose; but just as I was getting off the train a lady called me back saying, "You've left your coat, dear."

I smiled and said, "Oh, thank you." I put the coat over my arm and made my way to the ticket barrier where Mum was waiting for me. We caught the Underground to Brixton, made our way to Gresham Road and climbed the stairs to the top flat. I loved the throb and hubbub of

London. It was such a vibrant, noisy, smelly and exciting place.

The flat consisted of a small kitchen, a fairly large sitting/dining room (which Mum referred to as the lounge) and a double bedroom. The shared toilet and bathroom was on the floor below and there was a gas geyser over the bath for heating water.

Mum set to work, making a meal for when Dad came home from his job as an electrician at Hovis Flour Mills. We had a lovely meal while the wireless played and afterwards we sat and had a game of Monopoly.

The Z bed was opened up for me to sleep and Mum said, "Where's your nightie?" I went to my little case that I had put in the corner, under the hated coat. "What's that?" Mum asked, pointing.

"My coat," I replied, simply.

Her eyes opened wide. "But that's a jacket from a suit!" she said. I just shrugged. "Well, it's nearly June and far too warm for a coat!"

I was so relieved and, the next day, she took me to C+A and bought me a new dress, a new pair of shoes and a green blazer.

London was absolutely heaving with people because of the forthcoming coronation of our new Queen. We had made our way to Buckingham Palace and walked down The Mall. I was amazed at all the flags and bunting and decorations. A parade of soldiers marched along The Mall with a band playing. My head was spinning with the sights and sounds of everything: I loved it.

However, my Mum didn't like all the fuss. There were too many foreigners and she thought the new Queen wore too much makeup. I was shocked that she dared to criticise the Queen but nevertheless I had a lovely time, especially when we all went out on the motorbike.

Next day we stayed in the flat so Mum could catch up with her housework. She told me she had a recipe for a coronation cake and we could make it after lunch. We set to and I weighed out all the ingredients while watching Mum and listening to the wireless. She was a good housekeeper – the flat positively gleamed – and a great cook: the cake turned out beautifully.

The wireless programme was all about the rehearsal for the coronation and how particular the Duke of Norfolk was in making sure everything went smoothly. Mum asked if I knew who the Duke of Norfolk was - I hadn't a clue. She told me I should know as he was a very important Catholic and was the Queen's representative to the Pope.

She then asked me to get the table ready for the evening meal. I carefully lifted the glass fruit bowl from the highly polished oak table and unrolled the protective cover, before putting on the pure white starched table cloth and serviettes, and arranging the cutlery. Dad arrived home and we sat down for a lovely meal and I told him all we had done during the day. He said he had managed to get a day off work and we could go down to Sidcup to see Mum's parents next day.

When I was in bed later, I heard Mum and Dad talking in the kitchen next door. I heard her say she had an appointment at the hospital next week. I heard no more and fell asleep.

Next day we set off to Sidcup. Mum sat in the sidecar and I sat behind Dad, saluting all the RAC men on their motorbikes.

I had met the parents some time ago. Lindy and I went to Brixton one Whitsun - Alec was there too - and we went with Mum and Dad to Sidcup. I was very young and didn't have a lot to say. I spent most of the time playing with their dog, who was blind. All of us had a photo taken in the back garden. I remember that day very well: I must have been about 8 years old.

(From left to right) Me, Lindy, Great Aunty East, Dad and Alec.

This time, I thought I would try to join in the conversation. We arrived at the bungalow in Leechcroft Avenue.

"Hello, Phyllis; my, how you have grown."

"Hello Granny, hello Grandad," I said.

With that, Dad grabbed me and said, "You mustn't call them Granny and Grandad. Although they are your Mum's parents they are not your Grandparents."

I was so confused and looked at Mum to explain. Her mother stepped forward and gave me a cuddle and said, "No dear, I am not your Granny. I am your Great Aunt and you can call me Aunty East; and this is Uncle Fred."

What on earth was all this about? What the heck was a Great Aunt? I put it to the back of my mind but thought about the situation again when I was in bed that night. It still didn't make sense. Who could I ask? There was only one person, but she was not in my life anymore. I shed a few tears before falling asleep.

I arrived back at the convent by motorbike which was driven on this occasion by Mum. She told me she used to ride a motorbike during the war. I wish now that I had asked her more about her younger life but I never asked questions; I always thought it was rude.

Back in Bexhill, the convent was awash with red, white and blue paper-chains. The evening before the coronation, there was a special Mass said for the new Queen as she had requested that people pray for her.

Coronation day dawned, but it was very wet. We listened to the ceremony on the wireless. We were going to have a big party outside in the playground but because of the weather we partied in our large playroom instead. We sang and danced and played games and great fun was had with red, white and blue balloons.

I had asked Mum to save me all the newspaper cuttings of the Coronation. She sent lots on to me with a scrap book to keep them in.

There were lots of activities in the town that we were allowed to go to. There was a dog show in the carnival so we entered our dog, Shadow, and were bitterly disappointed when he didn't get a prize. We were invited to the Playhouse and Ritz cinemas to see films of the coronation and the conquest of Everest. We were also presented with a lovely little tabby kitten that we called Corrie.

We didn't go to Isleworth for our two week holiday that year; instead, we spent it in the mother House in Hammersmith. We had lots of lovely outings again: Windsor Castle, Kew Gardens, the Zoo and Battersea.

There was a television in the playroom - most of us had never seen one before. We sat and watched Bill and Ben, The Flowerpot Men one lunch time. We thought it was marvellous.

One day, we went to the local playground where a boy came up and asked why we were still in school when other schools had broken up for the holidays. We explained it was because a lot of us didn't have any homes or Mums and Dads. "Are you all bastards then?" he asked.

In complete innocence one of our girls replied, "No, we're all Roman Catholics."

The boy ran off to his, pals laughing his head off. Our girl had never heard the word bastard before, so she assumed it was some sort of religion.

I saw there was a swing empty so dashed across to have a go on it. There was a group of kids nearby sitting on the grass and having a giggle. I heard one boy say, "My brother told me this one last night." He went on to recite, "I'm in the Army now, they sent me to milk a cow. The cow blew off and I took off. I'm in the Air Force now!"

The little group rolled about with laughter and I thought, "That was funny, I must remember that."

We spent a lovely fortnight in that convent in Hammersmith. Back in Bexhill again we were rehearsing for Mother Helen's Feast Day concert. I can't remember the name of the play that I was in but I played the part of a pompous school teacher and I had to recite to the class, "In promulgating your cogitations or articulating your superficial sentimentalities with philosophical and psychological observations, beware of platitudinous ponderosity. Let your conversational communications and unpremeditated descantings have intelligibility, ventriloquent vernosity and vaniloquent vapidity." I was so proud that I could recite that without making a mistake. (Even though it's a sin I'm rather proud to admit that I still can, all these years later!)

There was a big tea party after and Mother Helen came to us to say thank you for the lovely concert. We were delighted, especially as she bought a large jar of sweets to share amongst us.

Chapter 16

August 19th 1953. It is a date ingrained in my memory.

"We're going swimming after dinner."

"Will we have our collation on the beach?"

"No, it's Wednesday. We have to be back for benediction."

"Oh well, hope the tide's out so we can play on the rocks."

And so after dinner, we all dashed to put on our swimming costumes (putting our knickers in rolled up towels) and then set off for Glyne Gap, about a mile away.

Sister Barbara and Sister Cuthbert (and a lady who I think was staying with us on holiday) accompanied us. as we walked in a crocodile line to the beach, passing the gas works and loitering under the railway bridge to see if a train would pass overhead.

We were delighted to see the tide was far out but gradually coming in. We quickly dropped our towels, took off our dresses and sandals and ran over the pebbles onto the sand. We had great fun looking for crabs and starfish among the rocks, chasing each other with long strands of sea-weed and playing leapfrog and hopscotch in the sand. A few of us could swim but we were not strong swimmers and so didn't venture too far out.

We spent a good couple of hours having fun and enjoying ourselves. It turned a bit breezier and a lot of the younger ones, feeling cold, got dressed and were playing on the pebbles.

After a while, Janet came down and called out that we must come out and get dressed. We reluctantly made our way to the water's edge. Janet called out to Catherine and Frances who were in the water behind us. Suddenly I saw Sister Barbara running down the beach towards us shouting and waving her arms. I heard a girl nearby say, "Oh my gosh! Look at those girls!"

I turned and saw three girls being washed towards the rocks. They were obviously in trouble with the waves washing over their heads.

The tide seemed to be coming in so quickly all of a sudden.

Sister was almost climbing onto the rocks while Cynthia and Ann were pulling her back and begging her not to go any further. I ran towards the rocks with Colleen following me. I jumped from rock to rock to where I could see a pair of arms in the air.

"There's one!" I shouted to Colleen but as I turned round, I saw her running back. I jumped onto another rock but didn't quite make it and fell into a deep pool where the water came over my head. I managed to climb out and saw Catherine just in front of me. As I was hauling her out, I saw Frances's terrified face as a wave washed over her. I never saw her again.

Catherine was able to walk when I helped her out, even though she was coughing and spluttering. I put my arm around her waist and one of her arms round my neck and then we slowly managed to find a way across the rocks. We eventually made it to the pebbles where a lot of the little ones were crying. Sister had moved a bit further along to where another group of girls were having trouble getting out of the water. I looked back at the rocks to see if I could spot Frances, but there was no sign of her.

I knew I had to get help: I let go of Catherine and ran up the pebbles to where there were a lot of beach huts nestled under the cliff face. I shouted "Help, please help!" I could hear Catherine behind me trying to keep up, but still coughing and shaking violently.

I saw a man and a lady outside one of the huts and again I shouted, "Please, can you help."

Suddenly, there was a rushing in my ears. I felt dizzy and fell to my knees as someone ran past me. Then I felt arms around me and heard a lady say, "Come with me, dear. It's alright. You are safe now." She helped me into the hut and someone brought Catherine in. She lay on the floor gasping and shaking. While I sat with my head on my raised knees, I felt someone put a coat around me and saw them put a towel around Catherine.

"What happened dear?" I heard a lady say. I suddenly remembered Frances and tried to jump up saying, "Frances fell back in!" but my legs felt very heavy and I promptly fell down again.

"Stay still, dear. Someone is coming so don't worry anymore." She handed me a mug of tea but I was crying too much to drink it.

A policeman appeared at the door and I thought I was going to be told off. I heard the lady talking to him and he replied that an ambulance would soon be here. Catherine had a glazed look in her eyes but she was breathing better. We were carried into the ambulance and wrapped in blankets. I don't remember too much about the journey to the hospital. We were put into a little room with two beds and Catherine said, "We are going to be in a lot of trouble because we are late for benediction."

"I saw you and Frances in the water: was Janet the other girl?" I asked.

"Yes. We were on our way out of the water when a big wave pushed us towards the rocks. It was so rough and we kept going under. We were all grabbing hold of each other, it was so scary. Then suddenly I was on my own and I felt the rocks. I kept trying to get out. Are Janet and Frances alright?"

"I don't know," was all I could say.

A nurse came in and said we were going home; the nuns said they would look after us from now on. I guess we must have been driven back to the convent but I have no idea who drove us. My head was spinning and I kept seeing Frances's terrified face.

We went through the visitor's door under the chapel and walked past the old ladies' department. There were lots of people in the corridor and I saw Alice and Monica. Alice took hold of my hand and said, "You know Frances is dead? And Janet is still missing."

It didn't register.

We were still barefoot and in our costumes with a blanket around each of us. We went along the Timber Passage and into the children's wing. We found our sandals and dresses in the changing room, but there was no sign of my knickers so I kept my costume on.

We made our way to the playroom where all the children were being looked after by Miss Cox. The juniors were running around playing and laughing. How could they play like that after what had happened? We went towards where the seniors were sitting, all looking sombre.

"Did you see Frances, is she alright? Do you know what happened to Janet? Nobody seems to know."

I repeated what Alice had said: that Frances was dead and Janet was missing.

They told me that quite a few girls had difficulty getting out of the water because the waves were coming in too quick. A lady had waded out to them and told them all to hold hands and form a chain, then she gradually pulled them towards her where the water was shallow. That way they got out safely.

Another group said they saw Frances brought ashore by a man and told how a couple of men from the gasworks were 'working' on her before she was taken away. Some said they thought she must have died. I was told that Sister Barbara kept trying to get into the water to help but she was pulled back by lots of kids who were scared she would drown.

Catherine was called out of the playroom and was told that a policeman wanted to ask her some questions. I closed my eyes and saw Frances's face again. I started crying. How could this happen? We had been bathing there for years without any problems.

Miss Cox came toward me and asked if I wanted to go to bed. I said, "Yes please," and left the playroom; I climbed the four flights of granite stairs to the dormitory.

I drew the curtains around my bed and got between the sheets. My head was thumping. I heard my curtains pulled back a bit and saw Sister Barbara standing there, her eyes red rimmed and swollen. "How do you feel?" she said.

"I'm alright, Sister."

She put a hand on my forehead and said, "Thank God we have one life saver among us," then she burst into tears and that set me off too. Another nun came into my cubicle and gently led Sister Barbara away. I could hear her sobbing all the way out of the dormitory, along the passage and through the door into the nuns' quarters.

Catherine came into my cubicle. "Was that Sister Barbara?"

"Yes. She is very upset."

"I've just been talking to a policeman. He is going to ask you some questions tomorrow. He was very kind. Sister Teresa was with me."

She started walking towards her bed which was the other side of the dormitory. She got into bed and I heard her say, "They are dead and I should be dead too."

I never heard the rest of the kids come to bed later.

I awoke to the sound of Sister Magdalen clapping her hands and saying, "Everybody up, come on! Out of bed."

We all got out of bed, stripped off the bedclothes and went across for our morning wash; then returned to make our beds and get dressed before going for morning mass.

It was as if nothing had happened. The only different thing about the mass was that we were asked to pray for Janet and Frances.

After breakfast, Sister Magdalen called me over to tell me that the policeman would be coming about 10 o'clock and that afterwards my stepmother would be coming to take me home for a while. With that I went off to do my morning work in the linen room. They were most concerned and they hadn't expected to see me for a few days. Sister Francis Xavier went to fetch me a cup of tea and some toast and, while she was gone, I told Alice and Monica that I was still wearing my bathing costume and my knickers were probably still on the beach with my towel.

They were horrified and Monica went and found me a pair from somewhere. She came back with a pair of pink 'directoire' knickers with legs that came down to my knees; what we kids would have called 'old fogeys' drawers' back then. It was a very kind gesture though, and I was grateful because there was a lot of sand in my swimsuit which was irritating me.

At 10 o'clock I went down to the visitor's parlour where Sister Teresa was waiting for me to see the policeman. He took out a note book and wrote down everything I told him; I had to sign it. He then told us that Janet's body had been found in the early hours when the tide had gone out. She was found face down stuck between two rocks.

Poor little Janet. She had been in the convent for as long as she could remember. No one ever came to visit her. Frances had a Mum but she didn't see her very often.

As I left the parlour I saw a young couple at the door unloading a load of books and toys and saying, "We are so sorry to hear of the tragedy." There were such kind people about.

I made my way back to the children's wing and joined them in the playroom. The juniors were laughing and playing as usual but a lot of the senior girls were sitting and talking, looking glum. I sat next to Pearl and she asked how things had gone with talking to the policeman. I assured her it had gone well.

She told me that they had been told off for not going to help Janet and Frances and had been accused of just standing by and watching them drown. It was so unfair but you just didn't argue; it was useless to do so.

We made our way to the refectory for dinner which we ate in silence. We only spoke at meal times if we were given permission. Sister told me that Lindy phoned to see if I was alright. Why didn't she write?

Chapter 17

Mum arrived after dinner but I was given a hurried message to tell her that she had to see Sister Magdalen before leaving: it was vitally important, apparently. We both sat in the classroom for about an hour, playing with Corrie the kitten. When Sister Magdalen arrived she apologised to Mum for keeping her waiting then informed us that there was to be an inquest tomorrow, 21st August, and that I would have to attend as a witness.

"Any other children going?" asked Mum.

"No, just Phyllis. She played such a vital role and we are very proud of her for what she did."

I thought, "What? First I've heard of that."

Mum said she understood and, after a while, asked what train I would be on so she could meet me at Victoria Station. Everything was sorted out and, giving me money for the rail ticket and saying not to worry about the inquest, she left.

Next day I was given a clean dress but still had on the old fogey knickers. Everyone kept telling me not to worry about the inquest. It would have been nice if I had been told what an inquest was and what I was supposed to do. I had never heard the word inquest before, but I never asked questions and just accepted whatever came along.

Sister Barbara, Sister Teresa and I, plus a few other people, all assembled in the Town Hall in Bexhill for the inquest. I was asked to swear on the bible - but before I could do that, Sister Teresa put down a Catholic bible so I could swear on that instead of a Protestant one. I was questioned again by a man about what had happened. I answered as best as I could and then signed my name.

When Sister Barbara was questioned she cried, which set me off. That poor nun was absolutely inconsolable and could hardly speak through her sobs.

One part of the inquest intrigued me though. I found out that both nuns had different names. I never realised that when they became nuns, they gave up their real names and took the name of a saint. I thought I must remember the real names and tell the other kids because Sister Teresa had the same name as one of the juniors.

At the end of the inquest, the verdict was announced - accidental deaths. We all left the Town Hall and Sister Teresa told me I should go and get some lunch. "Where?" I asked.

She pointed to a café and said, "Go in there and tell them you are from the convent and they will give you something to eat." Then she and Sister Barbara went the opposite way leaving me stood there not knowing what to do.

I couldn't go into the café as I did not have any money so I decided I would go to the station and wait for the next train to Victoria.

Just then a lady who had been at the inquest took hold of my arm and said, "Come on, dear. I want some lunch too. I'll come in with you."

She asked if I would like poached egg on toast. I said, "Yes please," although I didn't even know what poached egg was! She asked me all about life in the convent and I told her it was nice. I didn't know if she was anything to do with the convent and I thought that if I said anything bad about the place, I would get into trouble.

The kind lady walked me to the station after lunch and saw me on to the London train. I loved a train journey - I still do! - and settled down to enjoy the ride. I suddenly thought that I hadn't brought any other clothes with me: just the dress and blazer I was standing in.

Mum was there waiting for me when I got to Victoria. The first thing she asked was, "What was the verdict?" I told her it was an accident and she said no more.

We made our way to Brixton and the cosy flat. Mum lent me one of her nighties that night and took me straight round to C+A next morning where I was kitted out with a new dress and cardigan; then on to Marks and Spencer's for vests, knickers, pyjamas and socks, and finally to a shoe shop for new sandals. I felt wonderful and wondered why I couldn't live with Mum and Dad all the time.

Dad said we'd be going out next day and I assumed we would be going on the motorbike and was most surprised when he turned up in a car, a Morris Minor. We went to a place called Nun's Acre which was some sort of club in Goring on Thames (I believe). We had a meal and then rowed up the river. Next day we went to Sidcup to see Aunty East and Uncle Fred who both told me how proud they were of me.

On the Monday, Mum said she would need to go into work and that she would take me with her. We went to Farringdon Street where she worked in an office, something to do with the GPO. We walked into a room with two large desks and Mum sat me at one end of her desk and put a typewriter in front of me. She showed me the basics of what to do and gave me a magazine to copy from. I had a lovely time amusing myself on that machine.

Another lady came in and sat at the other desk. She said hello to me and carried on a conversation with Mum as they worked. I was so engrossed with my typing that I hardly heard what they were saying... but I did hear part of their conversation.

"It's definitely cancer," said Mum.

"Oh I am so sorry, Margaret. Can anything be done?"

"I have an appointment at the hospital next week."

A phone rang and that was the end of that conversation. We went to Lyons Corner House for lunch. I was just loving my time in London and. I am ashamed to admit that I hardly thought about Janet and Frances while I was away.

When it was time for me to go back to Bexhill, I really did not want to go. Mum drove me back in the car and gave me half a crown, which I hid in my shoe. She kissed me goodbye and said I could come home for a few days in the New Year.

Sitting with my friends again, they told me all about Janet and Frances's funeral; how all the seniors walked to Bexhill Cemetery with the nuns and the lovely white coffins the two little girls were buried in. I asked Catherine how she felt and she told me she wasn't allowed to go. She said the nuns told her that it would be too upsetting for her, but she wished she had gone.

Life seemed to carry on as normal. It was still summer holidays but we didn't go to the beach anymore that year. We didn't see much of Sister Barbara and learned soon after that she had left: she was replaced by Sister Macnise.

In September, one of the nuns (whose name escapes me) celebrated 50 years since taking her vows. We were given a day's holiday.

Pearl's grandmother came to visit and took me out with her two granddaughters. She was so kind to me: I felt I really didn't deserve it, especially as I had been so vile to Pearl some time previously. We had had another tiff (I can't remember what it was about) and she had retaliated with some remark... and then I said something really hurtful to her. I am too ashamed to say here what I actually said. She looked at me and her face just crumpled and she fled from me in tears. We never spoke for a long time and lots of girls told me that what I had said was really mean. I realised how bad I had been and eventually got her on her own and apologised. Bless her heart, she just looked at me and said, "Think no more about it." But that remark I made to her has haunted me ever after. I really did not deserve her as a friend.

Mum had written and asked what I would like for Christmas. I asked if I could have a writing pad and envelopes and perhaps a couple of stamps. True to her nature, she sent the parcel early but, because all parcels were kept until Christmas Day, I never wrote to say that I had received it. I had a furious letter from Mum to ask why I didn't have the decency to write and say 'thank you', especially as she had stamped a few of the envelopes for me. I wrote back telling her that all parcels were kept and that we would have to wait until the 25th - Christmas Day - before they were handed out.

As usual, all the letters were read before being posted and, when Sister Magdalen read mine, she literally exploded! "Have to wait! HAVE to wait!" she shouted at me. "Well, you won't HAVE to wait any longer." With that, she disappeared and a few moments later reappeared with a parcel and threw it at me. "Now you can sit down and rewrite your letter to your precious mother."

I opened the parcel in tears. What had I said that was so wrong? Why did she dislike me so much?

I sat and rewrote a letter on the lovely new note paper saying I was sorry for the delay in thanking her and how very pleased I was with my gift. I never mentioned anything about having to wait until Christmas Day for our parcels.

It was another lovely Christmas even though I had no parcel to open on the day: but I was content with what was in my stocking and the gift off the Christmas tree and I was more than happy to be included when a certain number of children were picked to go to the local pantomime at the De la Warr Pavilion.

De La Warr Pavilion, circa 1950.

After the show, we were given a tea party in the Pavilion attended by the Mayor. We would always sing a song for him and this year we sang 'The Last Rose of Summer'. It was sung in two parts and I was the one who sang the seconds on my own. I suspect that was the reason why I was one of the chosen ones.

I went home on New Year's Eve wearing my blazer. Mum took me to C+A and bought me a beautiful red coat with a hood and also a brown mac. We went to Sidcup to visit and Dad told me that Mum had cancer. I had heard of cancer but didn't know how bad it could be. Someone told me you got it by chewing gum too much but I never asked questions so was still ignorant about it all.

When I returned to school, I was told that all the girls over the age of eleven would now be going out to school, to Saint Mary Magdalen's in the town. Apparently people from the Home Office had visited a few weeks prior and thought we should mix with other children.

What? Did this mean that I might have to sit next to a boy? I was not very comfortable with that. The only dealings I had with the opposite sex were the old men in the convent and the priest and, of course, my brother Alec, a long time ago.

However, the following Monday about twenty of us walked to Saint Mary Magdalen's school. I wore my new red coat and was the envy of everyone; annoyingly though, Bridget started wearing my new mac. When I pointed out to her that it was mine, she told me that I couldn't wear both at the same time and anyway, "We have to share."

We settled in at school and I was put into Mr. Noonan's class. I sat between two nice girls named Jean and Marie, but behind me was a boy named Brian who kept poking me in the back and asking me questions.

There was a Mrs. Perry and a Miss Morgan who also taught in the other two classrooms. Mrs. Perry would take the girls into the playground for P.E. The 'outside' girls had proper navy-blue knickers in which to do exercises but all of us convent girls had old fashioned button-up knickers with no elastic in them. Some of the other girls were sniggering at us but Mrs. Perry soon put a stop to that.

We didn't stay for school dinner; we had to run all the way to the convent for ours and then run back to school for afternoon lessons. When we returned we saw a bucket outside: this had been left for the 'pig man' and contained the remains of the school dinners. We were horrified to see jam pudding and custard scraped on top of mashed potatoes and meat. Oh boy! What we would give for jam pudding.

It was no good: that jam pudding kept coming into my mind and I made the excuse that I needed to go to the lavatory. On the way there... yes, I am ashamed to admit that I did help myself to a big lump of that jam pudding and ate it in the toilet, complete with a smudge of custard mixed with mashed potato!

Brian would often lean forward and whisper things to me. One day he said, "Can I dip my pen in your inkwell?" I didn't understand what he meant as there was no inkwell on my desk, but Jean turned and told him not to be so rude. I still didn't get it!

A few days after being at St. Mary Magdalen's, I was called into see Sister Magdalen. "What papers have you been prying into?" she asked.

"I haven't been prying anywhere," I replied.

"Some of the juniors tell me you know all the proper names of the nuns."

"No. I only know Sister Teresa and Sister Barbara's names."

"So where did you get this information?"

"I heard it at the inquest," I said.

"Oh. Well... information like that is private and not to be spread about."

I went away thinking yet again, "Why does she dislike me so much?"

As I said, I was now a teenager and allowed into the Green Room. If I wasn't on the piano trying to pick out a tune, I would be going through the large stack of records. There were three or four by someone called Charlie Higgins who sang some very saucy songs. I would play them over and over again trying to memorise the words. Songs like 'Where the Violets Are Blue-oo and the Roses Are Red' and 'All Poshed Up with Me Daisies in Me Hand'.

But the one I enjoyed most of all was titled 'Mother's Walking Round in Father's Trousers'. I was trying to learn the last verse and kept replaying it over and over. It must have got on the other girls' nerves because Haven said, "Turn it off!"

I said, "I just want to learn this last verse."

"Turn it off!"

"No, I've nearly got it now."

Haven got out of her chair and walked towards me. She took the record off the gramophone and smashed it over my head. I never did know that last verse.

We would play games like snakes and ladders, ludo and snap, or read books, or play the piano… or just sit and talk. One day I remembered the funny verse I heard in that playground when we went to Hammersmith and I told it to the girls. They thought it was hilarious and, before I knew, every girl knew it. Unfortunately, one of the juniors told the verse to Sister Leonard who was horrified and wanted to know where the verse came from.

My name came up and I was in trouble again. I got the cane.

Chapter 18

Sister Macnise left and was replaced by Sister Fachnan, who taught a bit of needlework to the juniors and helped out with supervision. We were telling some kids at St. Mary Magdalen's school all about the nuns: some nice and some really strict. We said most of them had nicknames and we named some of them. Then we said we had a new nun but she didn't have a nickname just yet.

"What's her name?"

"Sister Fachnan."

"That's a funny name."

"Yes, that's why we can't think of a name."

"Call her fuckerarder," said one boy.

"Oh, that's so rude!" said one of the girls.

"Why is it rude?" we asked. "What does it mean?"

"Can't tell you that, but it is very bad!" Nevertheless, the name got about and was overheard and, straight away, it was assumed that I had something to do with it. I denied it and, for once, I was believed: no one was punished for it.

On Saturday mornings I still went to the linen room to do the cleaning. When I got there one day, the room was locked so I went to the old ladies' department to get the key. I asked to see Alice or Monica and was told Monica had just gone outside. I went out and was shocked to see her smoking a cigarette. I never knew that women could smoke.

I got the key and went and did my cleaning. Returning the key after a couple of hours, Monica was outside again with another lady and both were smoking. I went back to the children's wing and told a group of my friends that I had seen two ladies smoking.

"So what?" said Colleen. "My Mum smokes all the time and once she let me have a go." We were fascinated and asked what it was like. She bragged, "It was great."

After that, we all wanted to try it; but where would we get tobacco from? Sheila said, "I know what. My brother once made a cigarette out of dried moss rolled up in toilet paper." So we decided we'd give that a try.

We collected some moss and left it to dry on a radiator for a couple of days but, as I have said before, toilet paper was very hard to come by: and where could we get matches from?

Ellen, who worked in the church, managed to get hold of a few Swan Vesta matches that were used to light the tapers that, in turn, were used to light the church candles.

So… we had matches and 'tobacco': but what could we use to roll it in?

Someone suggested tearing a page from a hymn book, but we thought we'd better not: someone would be bound to get into trouble.

"How about a bit of newspaper?" someone else suggested. We managed to find a bit from somewhere and that's how our cigarette was created.

I put the 'ciggy' in my mouth: Colleen scraped the match against the wall and, as she brought the lit match forward, she said, "Don't forget, you must suck on it."

Before I had a chance to do anything, it just went WHOOSH! and the whole thing went up in flames, leaving me with singed eyebrows and a small blister on my nose. That put paid to smoking for me.

Chapter 19

Towards the end of January 1954, Sister Magdalen announced to us all that I was to be presented with a Royal Humane Society certificate for saving Catherine's life last summer. I was flabbergasted. I didn't think I had done anything special.

Sister said, "It is a great honour to have one of these certificates, so write and tell your mother and father."

I wrote a letter on my nice writing paper and it was posted the same day. When I received a letter from Mum, she said that she and Dad already knew because they had read it in the newspaper.

A couple of days later, I had two letters. One was from the girls at Ancaster House congratulating me on winning such a prestigious award. The other letter was from a man who put his address as 'Somewhere in Middlesex' and signed himself as 'Billy, aged 80'. With his congratulatory letter he had enclosed a prayer card and a £1 note. I was absolutely amazed that anyone would think of writing to me, let alone to send me so much money... I was even allowed to keep the money for myself. I still have those letters.

I was to be presented with the certificate by the Lord Mayor of Bexhill at the Town Hall. Some of the senior girls were allowed to come and see me being presented and around a dozen came with me and Catherine. The man who pulled Frances from the water was also presented with a certificate.

I didn't quite hear what the Mayor said to me because there was so much cheering and clapping and I was also distracted by flashlights going off. There was a photographer and a reporter there and afterwards we all trooped back to the convent where I showed my certificate to all who wanted to see it.

My picture was in the local newspaper, The Bexhill-on-Sea Observer, in the following week's edition (although they used my middle name by mistake and misspelled Catherine with a K).

Royal Humane Society
INSTITUTED 1774.
Supported by Voluntary Contributions.

PATRON,
Her Majesty the Queen

PRESIDENT,
H.R.H. the Duke of Gloucester, K.G. &c.

At a Meeting of the Committee of the Royal Humane Society held at Watergate House, York Buildings, Adelphi, W.C.2 on the 15th day of October 1953

Present: Roderick T Hawes, Esq, T.D,   in the Chair

It was Resolved Unanimously that the Honorary Testimonial of this Society, inscribed on Parchment be hereby given to PHYLLIS MARGARET FISHER for having on the 30th August 1953 gone to the rescue of several girls who were in imminent danger of drowning in the sea at Glyne Gap beach, Bexhill, Sussex, and whose lives she courageously assisted to save.

R. Hawes
Chairman.

Secretary.

The Mayor of Bexhill on Sea presenting me with my certificate.

The next day at school, a boy named Ivan came and asked me if I heard him cheering me in the Town Hall. I told him no, but from them on he would often come and talk to me at playtime.

Catherine's mother came to visit her one day and asked if she could meet me and take me out with Catherine. We went to the town and she very kindly bought me a necklace and bracelet. Later we went into a café for tea, during which she told me how hard her life was. Her husband had left and she was having trouble finding somewhere to live. I looked at Catherine and she was close to tears.

Fourteen-year-old Margaret Fisher (right) last week received the Royal Humane Society's certificate for her part in rescuing 12-year-old Katherine Cooney (left) from drowning. Both are pupils of Nazareth House, Bexhill. The rescue took place on August 19 when a party of the Nazareth House children were engulfed by a heavy wave while bathing at Glyne Gap, Bexhill. Two were drowned.

"Anyway," said her mother. "Thank you for saving her life. It was very brave of you."

When we got back to the convent, Catherine said, "I don't suppose I will ever see my Dad again - and I love him so much."

I gave her a hug. I knew what it was like to lose someone you loved.

The following weekend, Pearl's grandmother came to visit and again took me out. I began to feel spoilt.

Dad and Mum came to see me at Easter and I gave them my certificate to look after. Dad said he would frame it for me. (I got it back in 1986 - still unframed.)

To say I suffered from very painful periods would be an understatement. One day at school I felt so bad I almost fainted in class. Mr. Noonan called Mrs. Perry from her classroom and she helped me outside to the cloakroom. After a few minutes, I felt a bit better and told Mrs. Perry that I needed a towel. She gave me a different type to the ones I was used to. It was called Dr. White's and was so soft and comfortable. She told me to sit and rest until dinner time and then I should go back to the convent and go to bed. That sounded so good.

Then it was dinner time, I went back with the other girls and headed straight up to bed. I slept for a while then heard Sister Magdalen beside my bed saying, "So what's wrong with you, young madam?"

"I've got a bad stomach ache, Sister."

"Well, I'm sure you'll survive," she said as she left.

I lay there for a little while then got up to go to the toilet. I walked across the red tiled passage and into the three toilets. I closed the door and on the floor behind it was a stocking: not a lisle stocking but a lovely sheer one, like I'd never seen before. I guessed it must have been nylon although I'd never seen a nylon stocking in my life.

I put it on and stood admiring my leg. How glamorous I felt. I went back to bed with the stocking and lay there entranced by the sheerness and delicacy of it. I put it under my pillow and slept again.

Two girls came up later to ask if I wanted any supper. I put the stocking on and pranced around. "Where did you get that?" they asked.

"I just found it behind the door in one of the lavatories," I said. News of the stocking soon got about and lots of girls came up to see it. I swanned around wearing it, loving all the attention. Colleen arrived and asked where I'd got it and I told her. She said she had written to her Mum and asked her to send her some stockings for birthday. I thought no more about it until I was confronted by Sister Magdalen who demanded the stocking and asked how I managed to come by it. When I told her, she accused me of going into her cell and stealing a parcel that had arrived for Colleen (as the post arrived, Sister would take it into her cell to read the letters and parcels before handing them out).

I vehemently denied this - how could I get into her cell when it was always locked when she left it? She said I could have stretched through the tiny window that overlooked the beds in the dormitory. I was quite tubby and the window was only very small. I couldn't fit through there.

She then turned to all the girls and demanded the person who was responsible to own up. Nobody moved and we were told that all privileges would be stopped until the person responsible came forward. Loss of privileges meant not being allowed free time after supper and no sweets when they were available. This went on for about a week and I was getting evil glances and snide remarks. Colleen stopped me and asked what else had been in the parcel.

"How would I know, when I didn't have the parcel?" I said defiantly.

A group of girls then surrounded me and said that I must own up. I shouted at them, "It wasn't me." They said Sister could have left her door unlocked and I had ample time because I was in bed, supposed to be sick... and I was the one with the stocking.

I burst into tears and again denied that I had anything to do with it. Then they started chanting, "A guilty conscience will always cry, especially when they tell a lie!"

I felt so alone and unhappy. Nobody would talk to me, except Pearl. One girl ran past me and pulled my hair, shouting, "Own up, you thief!" I wanted to run away but where could I go? How I wished for my Lindy to be near.

After another week or so, we were told at breakfast that all privileges would be reinstated as the person responsible had owned up. Girls looked at me and sneered and I called out, "It wasn't me."

I looked to Sister Magdalen for some sort of support but she just said, "The person responsible has come forward so that is the end of the matter."

I was amazed. All I wanted was for her to confirm that it wasn't me but no: nothing. I am sure that to this day, there are people who still think I was the one. I looked over at Colleen to tell her again that I was innocent but she turned her head away from me.

I felt ostracized for a while with just Pearl talking to me. I needed to be in the other girls' good books again and I believed I could do this by making them laugh. Brian had told me a rude verse at school, so I recited it to one and all.

"Old mother Riley had a cow,
She wanted to milk it but didn't know how.
She pulled its tail instead of its tit
And all she got was a bucket of shit."

It did the rounds and things got gradually better but, unfortunately, Sister heard one of the juniors reciting it. I was on the carpet again when she was told it was me that started it.

"I might have known it was you," she said. "You are the lowest of the low. Hands out!"

Halfway through caning me, she lost it and the walking stick came down on me anywhere - everywhere! I yelled and cried and ended up in a heap on the floor. Then she made me get up and marched me down to the store room, opposite the green room and locked me in there for the rest of the day.

I sat in there and through my tears I realised I was in the wrong for reciting that verse, but all I had wanted was for everyone to like me again and the only way I could do that was to make them laugh.

I decided I had better do some good deeds from then on and hope Sister would think a bit better of me. She certainly frightened me when she lost control while hitting me. I ran my hands over the welts where the walking stick had landed and knew I would have a mass of bruises. At school the next day, I asked to be excused from P. E. because (get this) I didn't want Sister to get into trouble for causing the bruises when they were sure to be seen.

That weekend, Maureen was told off for not having her shoe buckled up. She told Sister the buckle had come off and was told if her buckle was not sewn back on by the end of the day, she would be caned. Poor Maureen had some form of deformity and could hardly thread a needle, let alone sew a buckle on.

I thought that now was my chance to do a good deed. I asked Maureen if she still had the buckle; she found it in her desk. I took her shoe and sewed the buckle on. She smiled and said, "Thanks."

Sister called her out later to see if the buckle was sewn on. "Who did this for you?" she asked. Maureen pointed to me and I sat waiting for a word of praise. "Well, you've sewn it on upside down. Do it again!"

At mass the next morning when Sister went to the nuns' choir to receive Holy Communion, we all started whispering to each other because there was nobody there to supervise us. The whispering stopped as soon as Sister reappeared. At the end of mass, the priest ordered all of us children to stay behind. When everyone else had left the church we had a fearful telling off from him about our behaviour in this 'sacred house of God'.

The telling off lasted about ten minutes and some of the little ones started crying. Needless to say Sister was not pleased and as we were walking along Timber Passage to the children's wing, she started yelling and shouting at us, "How dare you show me up in front of the priest, you horrible ungrateful lot. I've just about had enough of you all." With that she disappeared.

We were all scared and stood in the changing room wondering what we were supposed to do. Miss Cox soon arrived and took control of the situation. That night as we got ready for bed, we got Julianna to knock on Sister's cell door and apologise for our bad behaviour.

Sister said, "It's too late to say sorry. I have already written my letter to Mother General saying I just can't cope with looking after you anymore."

We didn't see much of her after that and shortly after she left for another convent. We wondered who we would get to replace her. I personally regretted her leaving. Even though she could be brutal with the walking stick that she used for a cane, there was something about her that I liked. Looking back, it must have been very frustrating looking after and teaching so many children. I know I am making excuses for her, but I always wanted to try to please her - just so that she would like me.

Oh no! We found out who was coming to replace Sister Magdalen Ita. It was none other than Sister Columba, the fearful nun who had charge of the seniors when Lindy and I first arrived all those years ago. There were not many who had been there long enough to remember her so we warned the others that things would not be better with the nun we were getting.

Anyway, we were not to worry about it just yet because we were swapping convents for two weeks, and this year we were off to Southampton to stay at a boys' convent. We couldn't work out how those boys managed to sit on those funny toilets stuck to the wall. Such innocence.

The liners Queen Elizabeth and Queen Mary were both in dock and a certain number of us were allowed a conducted tour on one or the other. There was also a boat trip to the Isle of Wight, a picnic in the New Forest and a visit to Beaulieu Abbey. I really dreaded going back to Bexhill.

Sister Columba was very quiet for the first week or so, but her eyes were everywhere. She seemed to be weighing things up. Gradually she started saying things like, "No matter how much you play up, you won't be getting rid of me." She would start on the older girls with, "Isn't it about time your people took you back?" When they did get ready to leave it was, "Huh! Your mothers dump you on us to look after you and when you're old enough to work, they want you back for the money."

It suddenly dawned on me that I would soon be fifteen and old enough to leave school. The school leaving age had been changed from fourteen to fifteen earlier that year.

I went home for a week for my birthday. Mum told me we would be going to Arundel in Sussex. "Do you know where Arundel is and do you know who lives there?"

"We went through Arundel when we were on our way to Southampton but I don't know who lives there. I remember there was a big castle on top of a hill."

"That's right: the Duke of Norfolk lives there. Do you remember? He's the man who organised the Queen's coronation. We are going there for an interview to see if you can work there when you leave school at Christmas."

I dared to ask a question. "What will I do there?"

"Probably housework, you are very good at that. You don't have any other skills. You never passed the scholarship and I don't think you would make a good nurse."

"When can I come home for good?" "You can't," she said. "Both your father and I go to work and, besides, no children are allowed to live in our flat."

"Silly me," I thought. "Fancy thinking you would be allowed to live in a proper house with people who were supposed to be your parents. Just do as you said you would - just accept what life throws at you. You are not worth anything better."

We caught the train from Victoria to Arundel and I was aghast when I saw the size of the castle from the train. It was much bigger than the view I had when we were on our way to Southampton. A taxi had been laid on to take us up to the castle.

We were met by the housekeeper, Mrs. Bovey, who did the interview. I must address the Duke and Duchess as 'Your Grace', and the four daughters as 'Milady'. Only speak to the family if they speak to you. One evening, one afternoon and every fourth Sunday off. Must be in no later than 10pm. Start work at 7am. Wages £6 per month.

"That's not bad," said Mum. "And what about uniform?"

"She will need two blue and white striped dresses and white aprons with bibs for mornings," Mrs. Bovey replied. "For afternoons she will need two black dresses, small white pinnies, black stockings and black shoes. Black cardigans can be worn."

We were given tea and cake and then it was decided I was suitable. I was to start a few days before Christmas.

A taxi took us back to Arundel Station and we then got the train back to London. Mum was very enthusiastic about me starting work in a castle and told me that the Queen and Duke of Edinburgh sometimes stayed there.

Dad wanted to know all about the interview and what uniform I would need and where would we buy it. Mum said, "Oh, it will be cheaper to have the dresses made than to buy them." And so, just before returning to the convent, I was measured up for everything.

Back at school, Pearl came to me and said, "I'm leaving."

I looked at her and said, "Why?"

"Me and Julie are going to Australia."

"For how long?"

"Forever, I think," she said. "My Granny says it will be the best for us. We are supposed to have two sisters there already."

I vaguely remembered two girls called Pat and Jean going to Australia soon after I arrived in the convent . I had been worried because I thought they would fall off the bottom of the world.

I looked at Pearl and asked if she felt excited but she had tears in her eyes as she said, "I don't know what to feel."

When Pearl and Julie left, I soon realised how much I was going to miss her and how bad I had been to her. I made up my mind that I would always keep in touch and stay friends. But then I thought, "Well, what do you expect? Every time you get too close or too friendly with anyone, they leave you."

Pearl (left) and I, with her sister Julie in front.

There was that feeling of rejection again and the thought of, "What use am I in the world?"

Then, "Just accept whatever life throws at you."

Chapter 20

We had a bad thunder storm one night and one little girl was so frightened, she got into another little girls bed. She was discovered there in the morning and both girls were caned by Sister Columba because they were both 'obviously up to low tricks'!

What was it with this nun? She hated to see two kids with their arms around each other. She would use the cane for the least little thing. She gradually got rid of a lot of the senior girls by telling them to write to whatever relatives they had and say they wanted to leave. If you dared to answer back, she would say things like, "You are nothing but a low bred cur."

I'd never heard the word cur before so thought I would look it up in the dictionary: but I looked up 'ker' and never found anything.

On one occasion, Clare was told she was a 'dirty bastard'. When we got to St. Mary Magdalen's, we asked Mr. Noonan what these words meant. He was horrified - but simply didn't believe us when we told him who had said these words.

Another time she said to us, "Do you honestly think that if abortion was legal, you would be here?" That didn't matter because we didn't know what abortion was.

Then it was my turn for the abuse. "I suppose you think you are it, just because you are going to work for Lady so and so." I never said a word. She continued, "Well let me tell you, madam, I know the likes of you. In no time you will be running around in a fur coat and no knickers."

I still didn't retaliate but, by golly, she knew just where to get me!

"I remember Lindy. She was a saint compared to you. There is no way that she is your sister."

"Of course she is my sister."

"I don't think so. You have blue eyes and if I remember rightly, Lindy has brown eyes and your father had brown eyes too. So you are just a mongrel."

I had never felt such anger and hatred as I did in that moment. I flew towards her screaming, "You nasty, evil black witch." In a flash she had a cane in her hand and she came at me, thrashing me for all she was worth.

If I could have got hold of her, I don't know what I would have done. How dare she tell me that the one and only person in my life that I still truly cared about was not my sister? I hadn't cried so much since Lindy had left. Just what was this nun doing looking after children? She had no love or compassion in her whatsoever and obviously had a screw loose. But it was no good complaining; nobody would believe you.

Next day at school, my eyes were puffed and swollen and I was still smarting from what she had said. Was it true that Lindy wasn't my sister? No! I would never believe it.

Mr. Noonan took me into his office and asked me what was wrong. I didn't want to tell him: what was the use? No one would ever believe that a nun could be so evil. The cane, the beatings, floggings, thrashings - call it what you will - I could cope with all that, but the verbal abuse was too cruel by far.

Chapter 21

"I'm leaving this dump," Colleen said.

"What, for good?"

"Yes. Sister wrote to my Mum and told her I was being a nuisance and a bad influence. I can't wait to get away from here. Can I borrow your red coat as I've got nothing decent to wear home?"

"Well, not really. What will I have to wear?"

"Oh go on, I'll send it back to you and after all you did steal my parcel."

I was furious. "I did not steal your parcel and no, you can't have my coat." She went off scowling and left when her mother came to collect her. I never saw her go, which is a pity because she left wearing my red coat and I never saw it again.

I went to school from then on wearing my brown mac which I almost had to fight Bridget for: she really thought she had every right to keep it.

Towards the end of November, I was realising my life would soon change. Ivan came and sat with me at playtime. He asked if I would write to him when I left. I said I would, if that was what he wanted. He said he would walk me back to the convent after school.

We walked back along by the gas works and just talked about nothing in particular. I realised that I would get told off because I was late for benediction so told Ivan I would have to leave very soon. He said goodbye and kissed me on the lips, then ran off leaving me at the bottom of Penland Road. I was most surprised: I had not expected that. Running towards the convent, my head was spinning. What was that all about?

Hearing the Adoremus being sung as I approached the convent, I knew I had missed benediction altogether, but I couldn't care less anymore. Throwing my mac on the outside window sill, I went and joined the rest of the girls, breathing a sigh of relief when I realised I had not been missed.

That night in bed, Clare went to open one of the windows. She said it was too stuffy in the dormitory. I heard her say, "There's someone trying to get into the playroom." She called out, "Hey, what are you up to?" and threw her slippers down two floors below.

"What's going on out there?" Sister Columba called out from her cell.

"There's someone climbing in one of the playroom windows."

"Are you sure?"

"Yes, Sister."

With that, she dashed out of her cell and ran to ring the police. We were all up at the windows looking down at the intruder.

"He's not moving much," said Teresa. Then I had a fit of giggles: that was my mac that I had thrown on the window still!

We saw the police arrive with torches and the playroom lights came on. Sister Columba came out of the playroom with a policeman and they lifted my mac off the window sill and picked up the slippers. With that I was called down to the playroom and asked to explain why my mac was there instead of hanging up in the changing room. I told them I was late back from school and just threw it there. The police smiled and said it was an honest mistake. Sister Columba was most apologetic to them and they left.

She turned to me and asked why I was late back from school. I told her a lie. "I had to go back for a book that I needed for my homework."

Standing before her in my nightie, she then asked me if I had been planning to sneak out later on that night. That was a laugh. No chance of that as we were locked in on that floor every night.

"I wouldn't put it past you," she said. "You're just a slut. Get off to bed."

I turned to go and felt a stinging blow across my backside. "Ouch!" I said. "What was that for?"

"That," she said with a smirk on her face, "was for showing me up in front of the police."

I ran toward the stairs and shouted over my shoulder, "You're a big fat bully."

I came to the conclusion that she must carry a cane in her large pocket all the time. Getting back into bed, my bum was on fire but I kept giggling over the whole episode.

As Christmas neared, I was getting excited at leaving - and yet I was tinged with sadness and almost fear. I received a Christmas card from Pearl in Australia but there was no address for me to write back to her.

A doctor gave me a medical check-up before leaving and said that I was a fine, healthy girl.

The night before leaving, I cried in bed. What was life going to be like for me now? I wasn't ready for life outside a convent. I could sew and knit and use a sewing machine. I could scrub and clean a lavatory. I could sing and dance and recite poetry. I could answer the mass in Latin.

Was that enough to get me by for life on the outside?

Oh well - just accept whatever life throws at you, eh?

Chapter 22

In 1963, my stepmother passed away from the cancer I had heard her discussing that day at work; my father married for the third time in 1966. For various reasons, I lost touch with my brother and sister: Alec had moved somewhere up north and Lindy was somewhere in Essex. I knew there had been some sort of disagreement between them and my father but didn't know the details.

I often feel bitter when thinking about my upbringing. My real mother abandoned me when I was practically a baby and it was fairly obvious to me that my father had no interest: I never once spent Christmas with him - not as a child nor as an adult.

My stepmother simply went through the motions and couldn't wait to offload me to a life of service in Arundel Castle, while my third mother, Pam, wasn't many years older than me. Three mothers and a father who I genuinely believe never wanted me.

Please don't think that I've never been happy though. I met Len while I was working at the castle and we married in 1961. Michael was born in 1964 and Edward in 1966 and they are both in long-lasting relationships with children of their own, so there is a happy ending to all of this.

In the 70s I attended my great aunt's funeral and met up with a man who said he was my uncle. In fact, he was one of my birth mother's brothers. He told me where Lindy lived and that she was always talking about me so, one day, I persuaded my husband to drive me and our sons to Southend. We found her house and sat outside for quite a while before Len asked when I was going to knock on the door. I just could not do it. I was afraid of being rejected again and I told him to drive off home. He was not very pleased.

Many years later, my Len got hold of Lindy's phone number and decided to ring her. I went and hid in the next room but he came and almost dragged me to the phone. I could hardly speak at first but then arrangements were made for us all to meet up in Southend.

I found that she was known by everyone there as Ros (her real name being Rosalind). I met her husband Jack and their five grown up children -

Sean, twins Christopher and Kathleen, Bernadette and Philomena. There was so much to talk about and I found out the reason Lindy had left the convent without saying goodbye to me was because she was told not to, as it might upset me: "And besides, the van is waiting to drive you to East Finchley."

I also met with Alec and his family: he married Molly, a lovely Yorkshire lass and they have three sons and two daughters.

When I asked about the upset with my Dad, it was because he had heard that Lindy and Alec were in contact with our birth mother in Canada. Dad was most indignant and Lindy in particular was told not to contact me any more as she was a bad influence on me.

Because of this, I was deprived of a lifetime of not being involved with either my brother's or sister's lives. My sons grew up not knowing any aunt/uncle or cousins from that side of the family, and for what? For 'parents' who seem to want to use their offspring as weapons.

Since then, I have made contact with my birth mother's Canadian family. She remarried and I have a wonderful collection of half-relatives in Alberta and Vancouver and the like: one of their sons flew over to represent them all at my husband Len's funeral in 2014 and, in turn, I spent a wonderful few weeks with them in September 2019.

I kept in touch with many of the convent girls and we would write to each other often, occasionally meeting up, even with those that emigrated to Canada, USA or Australia. So many of them have now passed on but there are a few of us olduns left and we've managed to learn how to use e-mail and Facebook, which saves us a fortune in stamps!

I eventually found my lovely friend, Pearl, via the Internet. We message each other daily and a few years ago she came back to England for a visit: in return, I've been able fly to Australia to visit her too. It was great to see her again and I apologised once more for the nasty thing I had said to her all those years ago.

Once more, she looked at me and said, "Think no more about it."

How I love that lady.

Phyllis Margaret Fisher.

Acknowledgments. I would like to thank Bernie, my niece, for converting my handwritten notes to typed text, and my son Mike for proofreading, correcting grammar and arranging for this to be printed/published.

© Phyllis Durham (nee Fisher) - October 2019

Made in the USA
Coppell, TX
23 December 2025

67210988R00125